# NONRESISTANCE AND RESPONSIBILITY, and Other Mennonite Essays

Gordon D. Kaufman

*Institute of Mennonite Studies Series Number 5*

FAITH AND LIFE PRESS, NEWTON, KANSAS

Library of Congress Number 79-53525
International Standard Book
Number 0-87303-024-9
Printed in the United States of America
Copyright © 1979 by Faith and Life Press
718 Main Street, Newton, Kansas 67114

Design by John Hiebert
Printing by Mennonite Press, Inc.

The Institute of Mennonite Studies is the
research agency of the Associated Mennonite
Biblical Seminaries, 3003 Benham Avenue,
Elkhart, Indiana. Other publications in the
Institute of Mennonite Studies Series are:

John Howard Yoder, *The Christian and
Capital Punishment,* 1961. (No. 1)

Paul Peachey, *The Church in the City,* 1963.
(No. 2)

John Howard Yoder, *The Christian Witness to
the State,* 1964. (No. 3)

Paul Peachey, *Who Is My Neighbor?,* 1964.
(No. 4)

# Contents

Introduction........................................... 4

Preface .............................................. 7

*Part One. A Mennonite View of Christian Faith and Life*

   I.   What is Our Unique Mission? .................... 13

  II.  Biblical Authority in a World of Power............. 20

 III.  God and Humanity .............................. 34

 IV.  The Church and the World ...................... 46

*Part Two. Nonresistance and Its Problems*

  V.  Nonresistance and Responsibility ................. 63

 VI.  Christian Decision Making....................... 82

*Part Three. Christian Participation in Secular Society*

 VII.  The Christian in Church and World................101

VIII.  The Significance of Art...........................116

 IX.  Mennonites and Professionalism..................122

  X.  A Vision for a Mennonite College .................133

# Introduction

*Even as Anabaptist* historiography *has moved from a single Zurich hearth theory of origin to a recognition of multiple roots, including not only lower Rhine, Moravian, and Central German soil, but also mysticism, spiritualism, and socioeconomic revolutionary roots, among others, so the* interpretations *of these movements have likewise been enlarged, changed, and challenged by scholars ranging from the so-called "Mennonite line" with its purported apologetic intention to the claimers and disclaimers of socialist and Marxist historians. The range of both historiography and interpretation of theological meaning has been wide, with the options posed at times complementing each other and at times contradictory in their thrust, but withal stimulating and fruitful.*

*The essays collected in this volume are a part of this spectrum of interpretation of the legacy of sixteenth-century Anabaptism and its relevance for contemporary personal, ecclesial, and especially social issues. They are being published not only as significant theological contributions in their own right, but also in the hope that their ready availability will contribute to and stimulate further dialogue about the meaning and relevance of truths for which men and women of a long gone age were willing to suffer and die.*

*Reformation leaders in the sixteenth century believed that honest debate could lead to the discerning of new truth. The many Anabaptist debates, though usually one-sided because the very lives of the debaters were at stake, testify to the fact that the Anabaptists too looked for new truth to be discovered through intense "dialogue." On the surface, dialogue about the issues raised in this volume seems less existential than the dialogue they experienced. And yet, if truth is immortal (Hubmaier), to enter into this dialogue can have implications far beyond personal growth and theological understanding, touching the very existence and future of humankind.*

*Appreciation is expressed here to Professor Kaufman for making these essays available and to Abingdon Press,* Mennonite Life, *and* Concern *for permission to reprint the articles published by them earlier, as will be indicated. The help and encouragement of the Commission on Education of the General Conference Mennonite Church are also gratefully acknowledged.*

*Cornelius J. Dyck*
*Institute of Mennonite Studies*
*Elkhart, Indiana*

*To Edna*

# Preface

For some time it has seemed to me desirable that there be available to Mennonites a more liberal and open interpretation of Christian faith and life than customarily appears under Mennonite auspices. We Mennonites have thought of ourselves preeminently as a Bible-believing people, and accordingly most of our publications focus directly on biblical texts and teachings as the proper point of departure for addressing any and every question that modern life raises. While this traditional approach often proves illuminating and helpful, it inevitably results in a certain narrowness of perspective on the one hand, and strained interpretations of biblical texts on the other. Narrowness of perspective results because modern experience and life are so utterly different from anything known to—or even imaginable by—the biblical writers, that it is difficult to do full justice to all the complexity and richness and difficulties of our world, when the attempt is made to render these entirely in terms of biblical concepts and categories. Strained interpretations of biblical texts result from the fact that the biblical writers were always dealing with problems and ideas arising in and from their own lives and cultural situations, and the parallels with our life and world are often distant and farfetched. Many persons, I think—especially younger professional people, well educated and living in settings quite far removed, at least culturally, from traditional rural Mennonite communities—feel the need for an interpretation of the Mennonite perspective which breathes more freely the atmosphere of the contemporary life and culture in which they are so deeply involved. They do not wish to give up some of the basic insights and convictions of the faith in which they were raised, but the only interpretations of that faith which are readily accessible often do not seem to address the questions and problems they are facing.

The present book will not be an entirely satisfactory answer to that need. It consists of a collection of essays and addresses written or presented over the past twenty years. Most are occasional pieces, produced on request or in response to situational needs in the Mennonite community which I felt called upon to address. I have put these together with several chapters from my book, *The Context of Decision* (New York: Abingdon Press, 1961; now out of print), which comprised the Menno Simons Lectures delivered at Bethel College in 1959. These chapters sketch certain main themes of Christian faith, thus providing a context within which the issues and problems discussed in the other essays can be understood. Though there are notable gaps and omissions, taken altogether the book presents a Mennonite perspective on life and the world which, although biblically oriented and grounded, is not tied in any way to biblicistic ways of thinking.

The main contention of the book is that the distinctive thing about Mennonites is their commitment to nonresistant discipleship, their emphasis on a way of life rather than a set of beliefs. Such an orientation, of course, is not obviously or self-evidently valid; it becomes intelligible and plausible only within a certain way of seeing life and the world, within a particular world view. I have tried here to sketch the conception of God and humanity, of church and world, of individual responsibility and decision, which seems to me to underlie the Mennonite conviction that it is in lives and communities of redemptive love that human beings find true fulfillment and meaning (salvation). I hope that this attempt to articulate the fundamental logical structure implicit in Mennonite-Christian faith will show that it is grounded in something far more profound and compelling than mere biblical authoritarianism. I hope also that this book can thus suggest a frame of interpretation for those who are committed to pursuing lives of nonresistant redemptive love in modern society.

The task of theology, as I understand it, is to work out an overall world view or picture of human existence which can provide orientation for Christian individuals and communities as they meet the ever new problems of life. It was in the biblical documents, of course, that this world-picture, with redemptive love at its center, was first set out; the Bible, therefore, is an indispensable resource in theological work. But each age must think through and sketch out afresh an understanding of life and the world which does full justice to its own experience, its own problems, its own needs. In the Reformation period, the Anabaptists, with all their variety and disagreements, struggled in a particularly powerful way with a radically nonresistant understanding of Christian faith. But their insights and interpretations, their convictions and claims, like those of the biblical writers before them, were worked out in terms of the social issues and political structures, the economic institutions and moral practices, the cultural experience and scientific conceptions of their own time. All of these matters have changed drastically since the first and sixteenth centuries—indeed, for most Mennonites, since the early part of the twentieth century. It is no longer possible, therefore, for us simply to take over the views of the biblical writers, or the Anabaptists, or, for that matter, earlier twentieth-century Mennonites; and it is a serious and highly constricting mistake to regard any of these as "authoritative" in the sense that we must "believe" them true. To do so is, to adopt Paul's language, to live under "law"—traditions and rules prescribed by the past—instead of in the "freedom [for which] Christ set us free" (Gal. 5:1). To live in freedom is to be open to what God is doing here and now, in this world and in this society in which we find ourselves, and to live in response to that activity of God. But that requires us to have the courage to think through afresh, from the perspective of our lives and our world, who God is and what God requires of us.

In this book I have tried to sketch out such a modern Mennonite-Christian world view, and within that context have discussed such distinctively Mennonite problems as the interpretation of nonresistance in the modern world, as well as more general cultural issues such as the meaning of art and the demands of modern professional life. Many other issues could have been addressed as well, but the intention was not to supply a full interpretation of all the major problems a modern Christian faces, but rather to suggest a way of working at these questions, a way which others can adapt to their own situations and needs.

Over the span of years during which these essays were written, my understanding of Christian faith and theology has changed in some significant ways, and in consequence not all emphases in these essays may be fully consistent with each other. The changes in my thought, however, have to do mostly with technical matters regarding the methods and foundations of theology (see my *Essay on Theological Method* [Missoula, Montana: Scholars Press, 1975]), and do not decisively affect my understanding of Christian faith as concerned primarily with forming persons and communities devoted to redemptive love. I now would not interpret the Christian life as founded so arbitrarily on an authoritarianism of revelation, as some of the chapters of this book written a good many years ago suggest, but would be inclined to argue the value of a posture of redemptive love as intrinsically right and good for humans (cf. Ch. 9); thus the heavy appeal to supposedly authoritative biblical texts would not find such a prominent place were I to rewrite these chapters today.

But I suspect that the more biblicistic style of these present chapters will not detract from the value of the book for many of its intended readers—indeed it may enhance that value by showing explicitly the connection of the ideas emphasized in the book with biblical views.

There is one feature of many of these writings which I definitely wish to retract: that is their thoroughly sexist character. When I wrote most of these essays, I, along with most other theological writers, was completely unconscious of the significance of the fact that in virtually all its talk about God, the Bible—and most Christian writers since—employs exclusively masculine terms ("Father," "Lord," "King," "he," etc.), and thus this language functions in ways quite oppressive to women. Moreover, the almost universal English use of masculine terms ("man," "he,") to refer to the generically human, compounds the problem further in much theological writing, including most of the present essays. Such uses of religious language contradict central demands of the Christian ethic and result in idolatrous conceptions of (a male) God. For the sexist forms of expression to be found in essays reprinted here, therefore, I wish to repent.

I hope the publication of the present collection of essays will prove helpful to those who, persuaded of the significance and meaning of an ethic of nonresistant love for modern society, seek an understanding of Christian faith which is Mennonite but not authoritarian.

*Gordon D. Kaufman*
*Harvard Divinity School*
*January 10, 1979*

# Part One:

# A MENNONITE VIEW OF CHRISTIAN FAITH AND LIFE

# Chapter 1

# What Is Our Unique Mission?*

On the night of 21 January 1525, in Zürich, Switzerland, a momentous event took place. A few years earlier Luther in Germany had made his break with the Roman Catholic Church and all Europe was in a great religious ferment. No one in Switzerland had as yet dared to break with Rome, however, though there was much discussion and agitation. But on this night an event happened that was destined to mean far more than simply a breaking away from the Roman Catholic Church and the spread of the Protestant Reformation. This is how that event is described in the old *Chronicle* of the Hutterian Brethren:

Conrad Grebel, Felix Manz and others came together and found that there was among themselves agreement in faith. . . . And it . . . came to pass, as they were assembled together, that great anxiety came upon them and they were moved in their hearts. Then they unitedly bowed their knees before God Almighty in heaven and called upon him, the searcher of all hearts, and implored him to grant them grace to do his divine will, and that he would bestow upon them his mercy. They realized in the sincere fear of God that it was firstly necessary to obtain from the divine Word and from the preaching of the same a true faith which worketh by love, and then to receive the true Christian baptism upon the confessed faith, as the answer of a good conscience toward God, being resolved henceforth to serve God in all godliness of a holy Christian life and to be steadfast in affliction to the end.

*From *Mennonite Life* (1961) 16:99-102.

For flesh and blood and human forwardness did by no means lead them to take such a step; for they knew what would fall to their lot to suffer and endure on account of it. After they had risen from their prayer, George Blaurock arose and earnestly asked Conrad Grebel to baptize him with the true Christian baptism upon the confession of his faith. And entreating him thus he knelt down, and Conrad baptized him, since there was at that time no ordained minister to perform such work. After this was done, the others likewise asked George to baptize them. He fulfilled their desire in sincere fear of God, and thus they gave themselves unitedly to the name of the Lord. Then some of them were chosen for the ministry of the gospel, and they began to teach and to keep the faith. Thus began the separation from the world and from its evil works.

This meeting of worship and prayer in which Grebel and Manz and Blaurock baptized each other was the beginning of the Mennonite community of faith. It was the first formal break with the Roman Catholic Church outside of Germany, but it went far beyond Luther's break with Rome. For the Mennonites—or, as they were called in those days (because of their insistence on baptizing adults who had already been baptized as infants in the Catholic Church) the *Wiedertaüfer* or Anabaptists, the rebaptizers—were not only attempting to break away from what they understood as the corruption of the Roman Church. These men were radicals who believed that the church needed more than simply reformation: it needed to be completely rebuilt from the ground up.

The church as understood by Rome—and even by Luther—was simply not the church of Jesus Christ and the Bible at all. For the true Christian fellowship, these men believed, consisted only of those who honestly and maturely believed that God had come into human history in Jesus Christ to transform history and humanity, and who responded to this act of God by consciously attempting to live a new life of discipleship to Christ. On this view one could not possibly become a Christian until one was mature enough to understand the terrible demands of discipleship to Christ and could thus decide to take up those responsibilities with conviction. The church was to consist only of those who had consciously and honestly decided to follow Christ no matter what the consequences. Since from the very beginning, baptism was the act through which one became a member of the church, then baptism could rightly be performed only upon the confession of faith and the sincere resolve to follow Christ as one's Lord.

This all seems normal and natural to those who have inherited this interpretation of the Christian faith from the Anabaptists, but it was far from evident to the church leaders of their time, either Protestant or Catholic. And it is not evident to many of our own time, for the prevailing practice in the Christian church has been infant baptism. Every person born into a Christian family was brought into the church shortly after birth. This meant that everyone was Christian, everyone was a member of the church, regardless of his own beliefs and actions. So long as he was a reasonably good citizen he was considered a good Christian. Luther had protested against many practices of the Roman Catholic Church and had insisted that the Christian faith must be focused on the Bible; but it was the Anabaptists who saw that biblical Christianity was the expression of the faith of adult believers. They insisted, therefore, that the earthly church should be restricted to those who in faith sincerely attempted to live a new life, a life based on the love and forgiveness of friends and enemies alike.

This understanding of the Christian faith led the Anabaptists to a number of important convictions not held by other Christians, either Protestant or Catholic. Since only adults who were consciously believers could join the church, it was essential for the church to be separate from the state, for the state included all members of society. The Anabaptists were thus the first to advocate separation of church and state.

Furthermore, it was evident that no one could be forced to be a believer. A person could become a believer only when he was convinced of the truth of the gospel, only when God had granted the gift of faith. But this meant that all persons must be allowed to study and interpret the Scriptures in the light of whatever guidance God gave them. No one had the right to compel another to accept his beliefs, since these were a matter between God and himself. Although the rest of the community would and should counsel and help wherever possible, compulsion in matters of religious faith was out of the question. The Anabaptists were thus the first advocates of religious freedom in the modern world.

A further consequence of the view that the church consists of believers was the conviction that every Christian is of necessity a minister of the gospel and therefore must preach and evangelize just as truly as those who were officially appointed ministers. The distinction between lay people and ministers was not of great importance to the Anabaptists; every Christian should be a missionary for Christ.

Emphasis on the absolute discipleship of every believer led the Anabaptists into a much more radical interpretation of the importance of Jesus' teachings about love than was accepted in the other churches. Within the church itself, all relations were to be governed by a spirit of love and self-giving to each other; there was to be no bitterness, hatred or animosity. The Christian church was to be a community in which each bore the other's burdens. In one group, the forerunners of the modern Hutterian Brethren, this emphasis was carried to the point of holding all property in common. But love and service were not to be restricted only to fellow Christians. Christ had commanded his followers to love even their enemies, and this also the Anabaptists insisted upon. It was, therefore, impossible for a Christian to become a soldier—or even a police official—for in these positions he might be called upon to try to destroy his enemy. He must, instead, attempt to serve the enemy and win him as a brother in Christ.

In the years that followed that fateful January night in Zürich, the Anabaptists had opportunity to demonstrate their belief that people should not return evil for evil, but should love their enemies. They were persecuted everywhere in Europe by both Protestant and Catholic authorities, and many thousands were drowned and burned as martyrs to their faith. For a time the Anabaptist movement spread like wildfire, but gradually the power of the initial convictions cooled, and persecution forced the groups to retire into obscurity. It is from the remnants of that movement that the present-day Mennonite community of faith stems.

What does it mean to be a Mennonite? What does it mean to belong to the church that traces its descent not back through Wesley, Calvin, or Luther, but through the Anabaptists? Should such a church be different from Methodist or Baptist or Presbyterian churches? Does it have a special treasure to guard and to give to the world? Does it have a special witness to make in the name of its Lord?

There were two things particularly that distinguished the early Anabaptists from other Christians. They insisted that one could be baptized and join the church only upon confession of faith. And they insisted that when one becomes a Christian, one's whole life must be subject to the Lordship of Christ. The command to love and forgive applied just as surely in a situation of war with an enemy nation as in a quarrel with a mean neighbor.

In most other matters they agreed with other Protestants. But where there were conflicts with these two fundamental convictions— as in the question of whether church and state should be separate, or whether a Christian could go to court to sue for his rights, or whether a Christian could be a soldier—they found it necessary to disagree. On some of these issues the position of the Anabaptists has been accepted by the rest of Protestantism, and even by Christendom as a whole. Thus, the principle of religious freedom has become widely approved, and most Christians would deny that the power of the state should, or could, be used to compel a person to be a Christian. In the United States separation of church and state is written into the federal constitution. In some Protestant circles adult baptism on confession of faith has become acceptable, and some of the foremost

Protestant theologians now teach that infant baptism is not justifiable. These positions no longer distinguish Mennonites from other Christians as they did at the time of the Reformation. They are insights our forebears gave to the Christian world at large, and which that world has increasingly accepted.

The question we Mennonites must put to ourselves is whether in these gifts to the Christian world, all that is of permanent value in our Anabaptist-Mennonite heritage has been given. If it has, then there is no longer any justification for the existence of a separate Mennonite community of faith, for our group is small and somewhat ineffective compared to others. Unless we have something special to contribute to Christianity as a whole, there is no excuse for remaining an isolated communion. To remain separate and independent simply because we have always been that way is for us to be the murderers who divide the very body of Christ—the church—by our own selfish sin. But, if there is still something in the depths of the Anabaptist-Mennonite tradition which is truly a part of the Christian gospel and the Christian life, but which others have not yet accepted, then there may well be an excuse for a Mennonite community of faith. If we have a unique role to play in God's work here on earth—a unique role as Mennonites who have, in God's graciousness, been given some special treasure to guard and to proclaim—then we have not only an excuse for existence, but a mission to fulfill. Then ours is a task which we, and only we, can perform, simply because of our Mennonite heritage.

Although some aspects of the Mennonite tradition have become generally accepted, the very heart of what the Anabaptists insisted upon is not so widely approved: that to be a Christian implies giving up everything in radical discipleship to Christ, the most characteristic feature of which is nonresistent love for one's neighbor and one's enemy. Modern Mennonites must ask two questions: First, is this radical discipleship of nonresistance a real and valid part of the Christian life, or is it not? If it is not, there is no point in our attempting to perpetuate it, for our business is to be Christians, not Mennonites. But if we are convinced that the Christian message makes the demand of radical discipleship on believers, then we must ask ourselves a second question: Is it not our special and particular mission as Mennonites to preserve and cherish and witness to this aspect of the Christian message which is either not understood or not accepted by other Christian groups? Has not God, by making us heirs to a tradition which sees the significance of these emphases, singled us out as those whose special task is to witness to this understanding of the Christian faith to all of Christendom, yes, to all of the world? No one else has been given this particular role to play, this particular task to perform, for no one else has the particular heritage which Mennonites enjoy.

If we accept the responsibility thus laid upon us, we are not thereby claiming that our interpretation of the Christian gospel is the only true one or that we understand fully and without distortion the whole gospel. No Christian has the right to claim such. Claiming to possess God's truth as only God can know it is making the idolatrous claim to be God. No, we must humbly admit that we "look through a glass darkly" even when witnessing to our profoundest convictions about the Christian faith. To witness to our convictions, then, does not involve the claim that these and only these are Christian truth. Rather, it means that we have freely and in faith accepted the particular responsibility God has laid on us as Mennonites, to do the task he has given to our group. There are many tasks in God's kingdom and he has many servants to perform them. It is not our business to perform them all, but it is our business to perform the tasks he has laid on us specifically through our own unique heritage. If we do not see this task—the task of being a Mennonite Christian, one who witnesses to the Mennonite understanding of the Christian faith—as our own, then perhaps our work in his kingdom could more properly be performed in community with others who see their vocation as we do.

But, if we accept as our peculiar and special role the attempt to live up to and witness to the understanding of the Christian faith stemming from the Anabaptist tradition, then certain obligations are laid upon us. In the first place, we must familiarize ourselves as much as possible with those aspects of the faith to which we are to witness. We must try to understand more profoundly why our forebears emphasized these matters rather than others, and we must seek God's help in trying to see the importance of the radical discipleship of nonresistant love.

In the second place, we must come to see that it is not our special task to witness to certain other phases of the gospel which other groups have as their own mission. Thus, while we will seek to appreciate what the Catholic tradition emphasizes as the sacramental character of the Christian faith, we will know that it is not our particular mission to witness to this. And while we will want to understand what Fundamentalist groups are contending for in insisting on the verbal inspiration of the Bible, we will see that this task has been given to other groups, and is not uniquely ours. We must not, of course, let our concern for our own witness exclude our awareness and appreciation of the work and witness of other Christian groups, for it is their task to inform us of the burden of the gospel which had been delivered to them. Nor should we shy away from appropriating aspects of the gospel preserved in other traditions, as if our own views were the only true ones and others need not be considered. But we must not dilute our witness to nonresistant love by fighting many other battles as well, for to do so will only result in our failure to accomplish the task which God has given specifically to us.

In the third place, if we come to see that our special role is to witness to nonresistant love in radical discipleship, we will want to ask ourselves again and again the questions: What does radical discipleship mean for a modern North American Christian? How does one manifest nonresistant love in one's economic practices? What kind of competition and pricing and labor policy is possible for one whose primary concern is to *love* not only friends, but competitors as well? What does love require in the political realm? Does it require me to withdraw from political affairs as the early Anabaptists thought, or does it require me to serve my neighbor through participating in politics? What about military service for the disciple of Christ? Is the historic Mennonite position the one to be followed here, or must a Christian disciple join the army? Finally, what should the Mennonite community of faith be in modern North America? How ought Christians to bear one another's burdens? How should the Mennonite community witness to other Christians and to the world regarding its faith?

If we are really concerned to take seriously the imperative to become disciples of Jesus, we dare not avoid asking ourselves such questions as these, and asking them over and over again. Nor, in seeking answers to them, dare we say to ourselves, "I would *prefer* doing this," or "I *like* to do that." The command laid upon us is to follow *Jesus,* not our own likes and preferences. Hence, if we would be Christians in the Anabaptist-Mennonite sense, the only thing that matters is obedience in every situation to Jesus' command that we love God and our fellow humans. No one knows all the answers to these problems. It is the duty of each disciple of Christ constantly to seek them out for himself. This is the task which God has laid upon us in making us heirs to the Mennonite tradition.

# Chapter 2

# Biblical Authority In a World of Power*

The juxtaposition of the concepts of "biblical authority," on the one hand, and "power," on the other, reflects the specifically Mennonite ethos and a peculiarly Mennonite problem. For Mennonites the question of biblical authority has been largely the question of what the Bible says about how we should live, and the answer to that question has been: Thou shalt love thy neighbor as thyself; thou shalt be a nonresistant Christian. When Mennonites, then, get out into the world of conflicting ideologies and presuppositions, the point at which they feel the sharpest challenge to what they have been taught from the Bible is in their convictions about nonresistance. After all, most others whom they contact also profess belief in God and Christ, but nonresistance is a strange doctrine, almost unheard of among Christians and non-Christians alike. That the world runs by power, and that one has certain rights and, indeed, duties, to exercise power over others in many or even all situations, seems taken for granted by virtually everyone. Whence, then, comes this strange belief that sets us off from our friends and fellows? The immediate and obvious answer to this question seems to be the Bible. It is a central emphasis of New Testament teaching, Mennonites have always believed, to stress nonresistance as the mode of the Christian life. Thus, to raise a question about the significance or rightness of nonresistance is, for a Mennonite, to question the authority of the Bible on one of its most important emphases, and thus to call into question the meaning and

*First delivered as a lecture to the Mennonite Graduate Fellowship meeting in Cambridge, Massachusetts, in December 1963; published in shortened form in *Mennonite Life* (April, 1966).

truth of the Bible as a whole. Or, conversely, if belief in biblical authority becomes weakened due, for example, to intellectual questions and problems which any reflective student is apt to encounter, the whole Mennonite ethic is threatened. Biblical authority and Mennonite convictions about nonresistance seem to belong together. What, then, can biblical authority mean in a world of power?

There are two questions to which we shall have to address ourselves in this paper. (1) How can a modern, intellectually sensitive Christian understand the notion of biblical authority? (2) Can biblical nonresistance make any real sense for a modern Christian aware of the power structures of society? Since the Bible is believed by most Mennonites to be the foundation for their ethic of nonresistance, let us consider the problem of biblical authority first.

## I.

We must immediately face up to the fact that the conception of biblical authority on which most of us have been reared has been relatively naive. We have been taught that the Bible is somehow the very Word of God, given that people might know who God is and how they are to live. Some of us have understood this to mean that the Holy Spirit virtually dictated the text of Scripture to the prophets and apostles who wrote it down and assembled it into its present form. Others have held to a more subtle—and probably somewhat more vague—doctrine of inspiration, according to which the authors of the biblical books dreamed their own dreams and thought their own thoughts and wrote their own words, but in all this they were somehow guided by God's spirit so that what they dreamed and thought and wrote would express that which God wills that people should know. The latter view, of course, avoids some of the problems every fundamentalism encounters with the prescientific ideas of the Bible and with the primitive and somewhat bloodthirsty morality of some portions of the Old Testament, because it does not require one to hold that every word in the Bible has to be accepted as somehow spoken by God himself. But both views in fact claim the Bible to be a book different from all others because of its ultimately supernatural origin and meaning. Whereas other books are merely human, this book in some unique way has God as its ultimate Author; it is the Word of God. As such, it is simply to be believed as the final guide and authority in faith and morals.

Theories of this sort about the Bible and about the foundations of Christian faith and life leave their adherents relatively defenseless when they encounter modern critical thought and awaken intellectually. In the first place, such theories, because of their insistence that we must believe certain ideas simply because they are found in the

Bible, conflict sharply with the sense of intellectual and moral autonomy which any awakening intellect must feel. As we learn to think, we begin to develop criteria of discrimination and judgment by means of which we do our work in mathematics or sociology, literature and physics. We discover that knowledge does not consist simply in believing what others have said, but in thinking for ourselves. The process of learning turns out to be the process through which we gradually become freed from mere reliance on the authority of thinkers before us, until we can judge and act in terms of our own sensitivities and creativity. We come to cherish the values of autonomy and to look upon every heteronomy as a kind of enslavement from which we must free ourselves if we are to become genuinely mature morally and intellectually. The new sense of freedom which we feel as we learn to think for ourselves is also a sense of genuine fulfillment of our humanity, and once having tasted it we can never again be fully satisfied with the immaturity of mere heteronomous belief. In the area of our specialization at least, where our intellect has been genuinely awakened—whether that be in chemistry or music, in psychology or history—we find it simply axiomatic that "the unexamined life is not worth living." Moreover, this awareness of the meaningfulness of moral and intellectual autonomy, once awakened, cannot be contained in some small corner of our lives; it tends to flow throughout. And so questions inevitably arise about the authority of the Bible. Why accept heteronomous authority here if not elsewhere? Isn't it necessary to think clearly and critically above all about matters of such importance as who or what God is? What is truly right and what wrong? Is it not, indeed, *immoral* simply to *believe* what our elders have told us here instead of thinking our own way through to the truth? Must not the Bible be questioned just as seriously and critically as any and every other kind of tradition? Thus, the very awakening of the critical spirit native to intellect, and thus necessarily promoted in any genuine education, inevitably calls biblical authority into question.

In the second place, when the Bible is subjected to the same kind of critical scrutiny which we have learned to apply to other documents, biblical authority in the traditional sense we have described becomes weakened further. For it turns out that the Bible, like any other book, is an expression of the culture that produced it. Though it contains historical reports, these reports are often in sharp conflict with each other and with other historical information at our disposal, and at many points it is necessary to reach the conclusion that the biblical writers were simply in error. In its statements about the world we live in, the Bible reflects the primitive three-story cosmology characteristic of ancient humankind—the heavens above being the abode of God and the heavenly host; the underworld below, the place of the dead and of the legions of Satan; the earth in between, a flat disk floating on the waters, the place where humankind dwells and the battleground between the forces of light and the forces of darkness. All of this, of course, has become completely incredible to the modern scientific mind with its belief that the earth is really but a second-rate planet revolving around a third-rate sun somewhere in one of the millions of galaxies which make up the universe—a far cry indeed from the very center of the cosmos where the Bible places humankind. Moreover, the Bible reports numerous events hardly more credible to a modern mind: axeheads which float on water, Red Seas which part so that a body of escaped slaves may pass through, an infant born from a virginal mother, the multiplication of a few loaves of bread into sufficient food for 5,000 people, and even the coming back to life of dead people. It is difficult indeed for a modern person, knowing what he does about the regularities of nature as science describes them, on the one hand, and the propensity of naive and primitive people to spin out and gullibly believe very "tall tales" (as seen in the records of many ancient peoples), on the other—to accept such reports at their face value when he finds them in the Bible. Indeed, the application of the methodologies of historical interpretation which are commonly applied to other ancient documents shows these stories, too, to be largely legendary. And so the relatively naive belief in the authority of the statements and ideas expressed in the Bible, whether in the more rigid fundamentalist form or according to some more flexible doctrine of inspiration-without-dictation, tends increasingly to shatter.

Most of us—however much we may wish not to admit it—have experienced in varying degrees this questioning and breaking-down of biblical authority. One can hardly pass through the intellectual awakening of a modern college education without beginning in some measure to ask critical questions about the Bible and its strange contents. And when those questions are once seriously raised and understood, it is no longer possible to accept the Bible's authority with the childlike faith of an earlier period of one's life.

Once the critical questions have been asked, what is to be done? It appears to me there are four alternatives. One can come to regard the Bible as simply another collection of ancient documents, interesting perhaps, but hardly the final criterion and guide for faith and life. This is what happens to a great many who find their earlier naive beliefs about the Bible no longer tenable, and know of no other way to deal with the problem of biblical authority. For such the Bible may well become a dead book.

A second alternative is to attempt the desperate holding operation which seeks to maintain the old belief about the Bible's authority by refusing to examine it critically. This involves a kind of compartmentalization in one's mind. One may be brilliantly free and critical in one's work in science or philosophy, but refuse completely to take up a critical stance with reference to any biblical materials. Instead of carefully investigating these documents and their meaning as one would the materials of one's professional work, such a person comes with a closed mind to any embarrassing questions, and seeks instead to build up rationalizations and defenses for the childish things he believes in what he calls his "faith." This alternative, of course, is simply the opposite face of the first one discussed: both assume that to give the Bible religious authority involves accepting biblical statements and ideas simply as true, however absurd they may appear to the modern mind. On this assumption the first alternative finds it necessary to reject the Bible as relatively useless to an intelligent person; the second finds it necessary to restrict the use of critical intelligence with reference to the Bible in order to retain some significant place for it. Neither alternative is very satisfactory.

A third approach to the problem, perhaps attractive to our Mennonite bias toward ethics, is to maintain that the Bible's significance is to be found primarily in its moral teachings, teachings which find their supreme expression in Jesus' Sermon on the Mount. From this point of view, it is of little consequence that on cosmological, scientific, and historical questions there are many errors in the Bible; we resolve to restrict our concern with biblical materials to the problem of right and wrong. Of course, this involves giving up much in the Bible which deals with other questions, but the claim can still be made on this veiw that the Bible is the guide to life and to living. The difficulty with this position—aside from the fact that it ignores completely the Bible's own claims about itself as somehow rooted in God's revelation and thus in a special way authoritative—is that it makes the ultimate standard for our ethical judgments ourselves, our own insights. For it is our own intuition of the rightness and goodness of nonresistant love that leads us to respect Jesus' ethic. Thus our own ethical insight becomes the ultimate arbiter of right and wrong, and there is no higher authority to which we submit ourselves and our intuitions for judgment and refinement. But this means that if and when we come to see that nonresistance or other teachings of Jesus are difficult or imprudent or naive, we will no longer feel obliged to give them serious attention, since only our own ideas on these questions really matter. Only if in some way Jesus' teachings are recognized as having genuine *authority* for us, so that when we find ourselves in disagreement with them we are led to question *ourselves* and *our* insights (and not peremptorily to reject Jesus' teachings)—only then can his teachings play a role of genuine significance in our lives and our thinking. But this forces us back, once again, to the general problem of biblical authority, a problem which cannot be bypassed by this easy focusing of attention on Jesus' ethical teachings and ignoring the more general claims of the Bible to authority in matters of ultimate truth and reality. We must, therefore, ask ourselves if there is not some other way to formulate the whole problem of biblical truth and authority than we have yet discussed.

What other way is there then? Is there some understanding of the Bible which both gives our intelligence free rein in seeking to interpret these documents against their historical background and also retains some genuine religious significance and authority for the Bible? In order to develop such an understanding we shall have to rethink the whole problem.

## II.

If we can try to drop our biases for a moment, and simply ask ourselves what kind of literature the Bible is, we shall see immediately that in many respects it appears to be a history book or a collection of historical documents. Much of the Old Testament reports what is alleged to be the history of the Hebrew people; the first five books of the New Testament tell the story of Jesus and the beginnings of the Christian church. Many of the other writings are commentary on or interpretation of these and other historical events. Thus, the prophetic books of the Old Testament contain criticism of the cultural and religious conditions of Israelite and Judean society, that is, they are interpretive of *contemporary* history and contain analyses and predictions of what is to be expected in the future if certain present trends continue. In the New Testament, similarly, the epistles are, for the most part, either elaboration of the meaning of the appearance, death, and resurrection of Jesus, or they deal with special problems in the fledgling churches. That is, they are concerned with interpretation of historical events either in the immediate past or in the present. Thus, we can begin our attempt to understand what the Bible is all about by seeing it as a collection of historical documents. It purports to be the history of the relations between God and humanity from the beginning of all things, through the election of a particular people by means of whom God proposed to overcome the sinful mess man had made of himself and his history, to the appearance of the man Jesus, in and through whom God was in fact transforming humankind and the world into the kingdom of love which he had originally intended them to be.

If we can agree that the Bible intends to present such a history of the relations of God and humanity, we are in a position to move toward a somewhat different understanding of its significance than we have thus far discussed. A historical writing has its meaning not in itself but in and through and because of the events it reports. Whereas we are interested in a piece of fiction because of its intrinsic beauty or meaning, our interest in historical writings is directed not primarily to the quality or even the content of the writings themselves, but rather to the *events reported in the writings.* These writings exist, so to speak, for the sake of the events, and their significance is simply that they are the *media* through which we come to know and understand the events. From this point of view, we can see that the problem of biblical authority has often been wrongly framed. It has been supposed that the real meaning of the biblical documents was somehow intrinsic to them, and the question was, therefore, Are these statements or ideas to be regarded as true? But if the Bible is primarily a history, clearly the real meaning of the biblical documents is to be found not in the documents themselves but *in the historical events to which they point.* The question is not, Are these biblical words God's Word? but rather, Are those events of biblical history God's acts? The Bible's meaning and significance, and thus its authority, is derived and secondary; it is in the events alleged to be the very acts of God himself that primary authority lies.

Now of course for a good many centuries of Christian history this distinction, however important it may be to us, was virtually imperceptible. For it was taken for granted that the Bible, as sacred history, reported exactly and in detail precisely what had happened from Adam to Christ that was of religious significance for humanity. There was no pressing need, therefore, to make the sharp distinction between events and reports which I have just made. If one believed the biblical documents, one came to knowledge of the significant historical events; and, contrariwise, all of our knowledge of the significant historical events here was to be derived directly from a fairly straightforward reading of the Bible. There was no question that what was said of Adam or Moses or Jesus in the Bible happened precisely as described. Under these circumstances it could be of no great importance to distinguish sharply between events and reports. With the modern era, however, and the development of new methods for obtaining knowledge of the past, this question becomes urgent.

When astrophysical, geological, and biological evidence and theories raise serious questions about the history of the earth and of life as suggested in Genesis; when archeological and other historical reports conflict with the stories we find in the biblical record; when careful historical analysis of the biblical documents themselves reveals such weighty inconsistencies and absurdities that it becomes necessary more or less completely to rewrite Hebrew history and that of the early church—it is clear that we can no longer take it for granted that the events which are God's mighty acts in human history can be apprehended simply through a relatively uncritical reading of the biblical record. For many of the events reported in the Bible did not happen that way at all, or perhaps did not happen at all. The assumption of a coincidence between God's act and biblical report, which led earlier generations of Protestants to suppose that their faith could be rooted in the Bible understood as God's Word rather than in the historical events in which God has acted, is no longer open to us for whom a gap has opened between actual historical event and biblical report.

In face of this problem what now can be said about biblical authority? There are two directions in which it is possible to move from the traditional view. One can say the authority for Christian faith is the Bible—and this will now have to mean the biblical *ideas* about God, Christ, and humanity, and not the actual historical events in which God is supposed to have acted (for, as we have seen, many of the biblical reports of events are inaccurate or false). The Bible then may still be called the "Word of God" in that it is the authoritative vehicle through which God has made known the ideas which we, if we are to be Christian, are called upon to believe. Though hardly expressing it in just these terms, much of neoorthodox theology and so-called "biblical theology" has in fact moved in this direction. Basically, we are called upon by these writers to believe the biblical ideas.

The other direction which we can move here is to maintain that the authority for Christian faith is to be found in the actual historical events in and through which God has acted. Doubtless much that is to be said about these events will depend on biblical reports—for where else are we given a history of God's dealings with humankind?—but it will not involve a simple and uncritical acceptance of these records. Rather biblical reports will have to be subjected to the most careful and critical historical scrutiny and analysis in order to find out, so far as this is possible, just what events actually lie behind the reports, for it is the *actual events* and not the reports about them that are the foundations of Christian faith and thought. Wherever it is possible to supplement and qualify and interpret biblical reports with archeological and other historical information about the past, we will seek to do so in order that the fullest and clearest picture of what actually happened may be forthcoming. On this view the Bible will retain a certain authority for Christian faith, namely the position of being the principal witness to the events on which faith is based. That is, the Bible will be our primary historical source document, but, as with all primary documents, its authority will be proximate and limited, and its reports will need to be criticized and qualified by such knowledge as we can come to of the events themselves.

It seems to me that, with the breakdown of confidence in the coincidence of biblical reports and the events of salvation-history, it is possible to go either of these two directions in seeking out a more adequate foundation for Christian faith. Since the first direction, the assertion of biblical authority in conscious awareness of the historical falsity of many biblical statements, leads to making faith primarily the act of believing biblical ideas—thus turning faith into a sort of philosophy or gnosticism rather than an orientation of the whole self—I prefer the second alternative. Selves gain their fundamental orientations from the crucial events they have experienced in the actual histories through which they have passed. If faith, then, has to do with the whole person and not simply his ideas, with the fundamental stance of the self in feeling, attitude and action as well as thought, then it must be rooted in certain actual events of history, not merely in reports about them. In the remainder of this paper, therefore, I shall seek to explicate for the problem of nonresistance in a world of power, this understanding of the ultimate authority for faith as residing in the actual historical *events* to which the Bible witnesses (rather than in the biblical statements themselves).

### III.

The Bible, we have been observing, is a history of the relations of God and humankind. Now it is to be noted that this is no ordinary history of two parties who happen to become acquainted with each other, see something of each other for a time, and then go their separate ways. Rather, the two parties in this history are of very unequal weight, for at the beginning one of them (humankind) does not exist at all, but is brought into being by the creative act of the other (God). Moreover, the parties never really become equals, for throughout this history it is only because God continues to sustain man in being that man continues to exist at all as one over against God, one who can enter into communication and community with him. Humanity's position here, then—indeed that of the entire universe—is in every respect secondary and derived; God's is primary and creative. It is for God's purposes that humanity and the world have been brought into being in the first place, and it is bcause he yet intends to achieve those purposes that God continues to sustain his creation in being and to work with and in it. The history, then, of God's dealings with humanity is really the story of the process through which God is realizing his intentions. Nonetheless, it is a genuine history between two parties because in his creation of man God has brought into being a creature who himself has the power to act and to respond, to create and to love, to obey and to rebel. Because he has made man in this way a free being, there can be and there is genuine intercourse and interaction between God and man as God works with man to achieve his intention, the creation of a community of genuinely free beings who can and do respond to him and to each other in love. It is to be recognized that God has not yet brought this history to its goal. The people with whom he is workiing have turned out to be rebellious and stubborn and intractable, and progress toward that end has therefore been slow and painful. Nevertheless, for those who know this God, who know something of his ultimate intentions and who know his love and patience and long-suffering, there is every reason to look forward to that grand and glorious future in which God's kingdom shall finally be realized.

The Bible now, as we can see, is the story of the meanderings and the struggles in this history. It opens with the creation of the world and of humankind and continues with stories of humanity's rebellion against God and refusal to be what God had created them to be. It tells of God's response to this continuing disobedience through choosing a special people with whom he would work in a special way in order to, at last, bring all humankind round to obedience of his will and thus genuine fulfillment. It details the unfaithfulness of this people, the children of Israel, and God's reaction to that, involving finally the destruction of the two Hebrew kingdoms and the carrying off of the people into exile, but involving also the sending of prophets or spokesmen who could interpret to the people the real meaning of those unhappy events. It relates, finally, the story of how, after centuries of preparation of this people, "when the time had fully come" (as Paul put it), "God sent forth his Son" (Gal. 4:4) in order finally to make plain who he is and what his will is, and in this way established a community, the church, in which his spirit of love was alive and at work within history itself. It is this community which knows God's spirit and his love, naturally enough, for whom the Bible is the real history of man and his dealings with his Creator. It is this community, therefore, which has cherished the Old Testament of Jewish Scriptures and written the New Testament to relate and interpret the great events surrounding Jesus of Nazareth. It is this community which looks forward to the final achievement of God's purposes in what the seer of Revelation called "a new heaven and a new earth, . . . [a] new Jerusalem, . . . [in which at last] the dwelling of God is with men" (Rev. 21:1-3, RSV).

Now it is in the context of this historical movement which has its beginning with God's act to bring a world and man into being, which moves gradually toward a central point in Jesus Christ in and through whom the meaning of the whole of history and the purposes of God for history come into human view, which can be expected finally to reach its culmination and climax in the full establishment of the kingdom of God—it is in the context of this historical movement involving all creation that we must ask the questions: What ought we to do? What is the right?

It should be clear that the answers to these questions—given the premise of Christian faith that God is really moving all creation through a history which will finally culminate in the realization of his purposes—are to be found wholly and exclusively in the will of God and in the character of the kingdom toward which he is moving us. If it were the case that man were alone in the universe, responsible to no higher will than his own, or if God were not a historical God who has brought the world into being to realize certain objectives and who is even now acting to transform this world and man so that those objectives will be fulfilled, then our ethics might find some other basis. Perhaps we might base it in human need or human pleasures or human desires; perhaps we might develop a rational or a utilitarian ethic, or one founded in the human sense of duty or virtue or in the human appreciation of value. But for the Christian understanding that we are in a history which is actually going some place, and that we have been placed here intentionally so that the purposes of God to achieve his kingdom might be realized, these other bases for ethics become irrelevant. The only proper consideration is, where in fact is history going? what is its goal? and how do we fit into this movement? If we can find our proper place within the inexorable movement, we shall find such fulfillment of our beings as is open to us, and our lives will enjoy real meaningfulness; if not, we shall always be frustrated and unhappy and insecure, square pegs in round holes. It is of decisive importance, therefore, if the Christian understanding of humankind and history are true, for us to come to some genuine insight into the nature of the kingdom which God is ushering in and the methods through which he is accomplishing this, his end.

For Christian faith such knowledge is available, not in the form of truths to be learned from the Bible or elsewhere, but in the form of an event exemplifying at once God's ends and his methods, the event which we call the appearance, death, and resurrection of Jesus Christ. For Christian faith this event—particularly the self-giving and suffering of Jesus' passion and death—is the outstanding example and expression of the redemptive love which characterizes God's kingdom and which is the means through which God is transforming the chaos of present human existence into his kingdom. This event, then, of self-sacrifice and self-giving, of bearing whatever burdens others cast upon him, of refusing to resist those who were evil, but turning instead the other cheek (Mt. 5:39), of refusing to revile in return those who had reviled him (1 Pet. 2:23)—this event exemplifying and expressing in a concrete way actual love for actual enemies is the paradigm or model which defines right action for Christian faith. For in and through this event we see that God himself is one who conquers not by overwhelming power but by overwhelming love; and his kingdom is no tyrannical kingdom of terror, but a compassionate kingdom of love. Little wonder that the cross has always been the supreme symbol of Christian faith!

However, if we take seriously the meaning of that symbol for ethics, we must say that the life to which we are called is life in the same kingdom of love under the sovereignty of the same God of love, a life and a love which manifest themselves in this world not by threat or hate or power, but by self-giving and nonresistant redemptive love. "Have this mind among yourselves," said Paul, "which is yours in Christ Jesus, who . . . emptied himself, taking the form of a servant . . . and became obedient unto death" (Phil. 2:5-8, RSV). ". . . Christ . . . suffered for you," says Peter, "leaving you an example, that you should follow in his steps. . . . When he was reviled, he did not revile in return; when he suffered, he did not threaten; but he trusted to him who judges justly" (1 Pet. 2:21, 23, RSV). "In this is love," says John, "not that we loved God but that he loved us and sent his Son to be the expiation for our sins. Beloved, if God so loved us, we also ought to love one another" (1 Jn. 4:10, 11, RSV). This understanding of what is required of the Christian, drawn from the powerful example of Jesus' cross, is of course fully consonant with Jesus' own teaching:

"But I say to you that hear, Love your enemies, do good to those who hate you, bless those who curse you, pray for those who abuse you. . . . If you love those who love you, what credit is that to you? For even sinners love those who love them. And if you do good to those who do good to you, what credit is that to you? For even sinners do the same. And if you lend to those from whom you hope to receive, what credit is that to you? Even sinners lend to sinners, to receive as much again. But love your enemies, and do good, and lend, expecting nothing in return; and your reward will be great, and you will be sons of the Most High; for he is kind to the ungrateful and the selfish. Be merciful, even as your Father is merciful" (Lk. 6:27-28, 32-36, RSV).

What, now, are we to make of this demand that we lead lives of nonresistant love in the world in which we live, a world governed by power and powers? The answer should be clear. Such self-giving and self-sacrificial action is all that makes real sense in our world. It does not make sense, of course, in terms of worldly standards. For there is little evidence that such action gets one ahead in the world, or brings one wealth or prestige or power, or even happiness or friendship. In its outstanding exemplification it brought death on a cross, shame and public ridicule, scorn of enemies and desertion by friends. There is no particular reason why we should believe in or hope for anything better. What we know of gas chambers and brainwashing and atomic bombs can hardly lead us to suppose that the character of the world and the people in it have changed materially for the better since Jesus' time. Nonetheless, I repeat, this sort of life and this model of action makes real sense. It does, that is, on the Christian presupposition that God has actually created this world to establish his kingdom of love and that even now he is acting in this world to usher in that realm—that, in fact, it is precisely through just such self-sacrificing love that he is acting to transform the chaos of evil and hate in which we live into his perfect kingdom. If the course of history is really under God's sovereignty, and if his sovereignty over the human heart is really achieved and exercised precisely through such redemptive love, and if in this way he is in fact bringing our history into the perfect community of love he created it for—and these are very big "if's" indeed!—then surely right action can be understood only in terms of finding our proper places within this actual historical movement toward the redemption of all history. For it is this movement that is the real meaning of history, and it is this movement which shall finally overcome all others in history. It is in and through this movement that the ultimate reality with which we have to do—God himself—is present and active, and it is here, therefore, and here alone, that we can find such reality and fulfillment as is open to us. To find our place, not among spurious or false historical movements, but within the central reality of the historical process—that is to have life and to have it in abundance. To live, thus, in response to what is revealed in the cross, is to live the only life which makes genuine sense, even in a world of power. But the Christian ethic makes such sense, not to any pragmatic or prudential or rational analysis of experience, but only in light of the Christian eschatological hope for the actual coming of God's perfect kingdom.

## IV.

We began this paper with a question about how biblical authority is to be understood in the world of power in which we live. I have tried to show that there is no easy answer to this question, because, in the light of our modern understanding of the world and the Bible, it is necessary to reformulate completely the conception of biblical authority. No longer is it possible to regard the Bible as possessing a kind of intrinsic or inherent authority which faith may or must accept. On the contrary, such authority as the Bible has, I have argued, lies in the fact that it is the primary document reporting the history which we must know if we are to understand ourselves and our world. Its authority is derivative from the actual historical events through which God is bringing creation to the end for which he originally created it, and it is this movement of history from creation to consummation which is of primary interest to Christian faith, not the Bible as such. Since Jesus' crucifixion is, for Christian faith, the event in which this underlying movement of the historical process becomes both visible and decisively effective in the actual transformation of history, it is to this event above all that we must look in seeking to understand both ourselves and what is required of us and also the significance of the world of power in which we live. In this event Christian faith believes it sees into the very heart of God. Here, then, is encountered the ultimate authority for Christian faith, God himself. Here must be the source of all norms for Christian ethics. Since this event, understood in this way, reveals suffering love to be the ultimate power in the universe, the power which shall overcome all other powers which now seem to control our world, it is in terms of and as expressive of such suffering and redemptive love that we are called to live—even in this world which, superficially viewed, appears to be ruled by force and power. For we are called to live in this world, "not by might, nor by power, but by my Spirit, says the Lord of hosts" (Zech. 4:6, RSV).

# Chapter 3

# God and Humanity*

A distinctive characteristic of the Christian perspective is the understanding that man has his very being in community with God and his fellows, a community strained toward disruption by man's acts of distrust and disobedience, yet healed by God's acts of love and reconciliation. This summary statement may seem obvious enough, but not so obvious are some of its implications for the nature of man and his relation to God. For it is implied here that man's being is in some significant way determined by events, that is, that man's very nature is historical, that to grasp what any man is, we must look at his history.

I.

The meaning of this will come clearer if we reflect briefly on our actual relations with other persons. Those relations always have their character in the present because of what they have been in the past. For example, if I call someone my friend and take up a stance of trust and openness toward him, this does not happen because of my arbitrary decision in this moment to be a friend of this person. I do not find myself easily and freely trusting, say, a perfect stranger. If I have a friend, it is because I have *come* to have a friend; it is because, through a series of encounters with this other person in the past, I have gradually become acquainted with him, and he with me, and between us has arisen the relational reality which we call friendship. My friendship for another is thus something that arises out of the

*From *The Context of Decision* (New York: Abingdon Press, 1961), pp. 30-47.

*history* of my relations with that other. Precisely the same thing is to be said of an enemy. If I call someone my enemy, it is because my encounters with that person have, far from maturing into friendship, matured into distrust and fear and hatred. But these realities, like friendship, have come to be what they now are through a process of development, through a history. And given a different historical development, the present relationships would be different realities.

It is important that we grasp a further point here. These relations of friendship and enmity in which we stand are not completely external to us, leaving us untouched in the innermost core of our beings. On the contrary, it is just such relationships that, in many respects, have made us what we are. As I share experiences with my friend, and he with me, we come to appreciate the aspirations, the desires, the values of each other. It is because my friend finds real joy and satisfaction in good music, or philosophy, or football, that he wishes me, too, to share these experiences. And so together with my friend I taste of realities I had not known before, and soon, perhaps, I share his appreciation and joy. But this sharing occurs not only with regard to new types of experience. In our every conversation we are really exchanging experiences of the world and attitudes toward the world, and are thus coming to apprehend the world in new ways, taking up new postures toward it. My friend comes to participate in my values, attitudes, ideas, and ideals, and I in his. In short, we come to participate in each other; we become, in Paul's words, "members one of another" (Rom. 12;5); the very structures of our selves come to interpenetrate each other in such a way that I am what I am because he is what he is, and because of the relationship we have come to enjoy together. Similarly, one must argue that the experiences of injury and betrayal which have given rise to relationships of distrust, fear, and enmity, are not external to my true self; they also have left their scars on what I now am; they also have shaped the structure of my self.

What we have said about friendship and enmity applies to all relationships in which we stand or have stood, relations to things as well as persons. The self is that unique kind of reality which lives in continuous responsiveness to other realities in the present, but whose very structure, from which the responses emerge, has come to be what it is because of its past. *We are our histories.* Hence, the study of history is really the unraveling backward through time of the present structures of selves, in such a way that we can see how they have come to interpenetrate each other.

The self gains its structure through history, but it is a vital and responsive reality in the present, and these two facts belong together. For to be *responsive* to another is to be one who makes himself sensitive to that other, who hears when the other speaks and who replies with relevance to what the other has said. That is, it is to be the kind of being that can adapt itself relevantly and significantly to the other reality confronting it; it is to be the kind of being that can allow itself to be shaped by the living experience of the present into some form which would not otherwise have been taken. To be responsive is, in short, to be a being for whom every present moment is a shaping moment, and thus for whom every past moment was one in which I *was* shaped, in which I was coming to have the structure which I now have. To deny that the self gains its structure through history would be to deny that it is the kind of reality which can enter into living dialogue in the present. Man's historicity—his being shaped by history—and man's finding his very being in community with others thus are two sides of the same coin; neither could be without the other.

Just as history is the present structure of the self unravelled backward through time, so community is that structure unfolded outward so as to lay bare the interpenetration and permeation of the self with others. Thus, to speak of the communities in which we participate is to refer to the living relations to other persons which actually constitute our present being; to speak of the vital relations to other selves in which we stand is to designate the communities of which we are part. Communities are nothing but selves in living relation; selves have their very being in and through the communal relations in which they stand. Community—self—history: these are the three terms of a complex triadic relationship, none of which could exist apart from the others. Accordingly, the nature and problems of the community among people, and between humankind and God, must be seen from three sides if they are to be properly understood. They will have their historical dimension through which they came to be what they are; they will have their personal dimension in which they must be grasped in terms of the structure and malformation of individual selves; they will have their social dimension in which we will see them as the structures and tensions in society and culture.

## II.

Although in developing this triadic conception of the relations of the individual, the community, and history, direct exegesis of biblical passages has not been attempted, the conception itself is directly implied in the Bible and Christian theology. For the Bible is essentially a history in and through which we can see how the situations of individual and community, each indispensable to the other, have become what they are. Moreover, it is only in terms of some such anthropology as here outlined that we can make intelligible the doctrines of the fall and sin on the one hand, and of salvation through Jesus Christ on the other. For in each of these, the claim is being made that some event in history radically shapes—in the one case for the worse, in the other for the better—our present situation.

The biblical story of the fall has many implications which we cannot explore here. However, we must note at least these two: (a) The story insists that our present involvement in evil has come to us out of history, out of the past. (b) The past with which we are here concerned is not merely our particular past as Americans or as Christians; it is the general human past to which all men are heir. This is emphasized through making Adam, the symbolic progenitor of all people, the one through whom sinful disobedience came into human affairs.

> In Adam's fall
> We sinned all.

The evidence for these claims is so obvious that it scarcely needs rehearsing. At every level of human intercourse distrust, hatred, and fear rule the relations of people. This is certainly true, for example, on the international scene where every nation is clearly out to save itself in the full confidence that it can trust no other. It is equally true of the relations between white and black both within this country and across the globe, of the relations between capital and labor, between the "masses" and the "eggheads," between Southerners and Northerners, between Protestants and Catholics and Jews. Moreover, if we are honest, we must admit that our personal relations likewise are filled with often hidden, but sometimes open, distrust and hatred. All parents find moments when they cannot stand the sight of their child, and even in better moments they are subject to the temptation to use and manipulate the child simply for their own ends. Children grow up in a family atmosphere where they must continually vie for the affection of parents and playmates. No employer hesitates to use the threat of dismissal even with employees whom he claims as friends, and wages and prices are never fixed on the basis of love for all parties involved. In every church, whatever its claims to be a community of love, there are bitter jealousies, hatreds, and struggles for power and influence. I need not go on. What I am referring to is familiar to all. Our lives and our very selves are filled at every point with poisons of distrust and fear. Who of us is confident enough of the love of any person to be willing to bare absolutely and completely every innermost thought or secret? Each of us maintains a hard protective shell against every other human for fear we might be hurt should this or that secret fault or weakness which we alone know be discovered.

Now it is this fact—that human relations at every level simply are not what they ought to be—that is pointed to by the Christian doctrine of sin. That aspect of the doctrine referred to as the fall expresses the insight that we have made our communities and selves the corrupted and destructive realities they are, not just in this moment, but through history. And it is a history which ultimately includes in its corruption all people all the way back to the beginnings of the species.

On every level this is the case. Our present international problems are not just willed deliberately into being by irresponsible Communists or Americans. They are the product of a long series of events and crises stretching back through World War II, the depression, the Versailles Treaty, the Communist revolution in Russia, World War I, nineteenth-century imperialism and colonialism, the industrial revolution, and so on back to the very beginning of history. Each of these moments, though creative and productive in its own right, was shaped by the hatreds, jealousies, rivalries, and distrust which its participants held for each other. We should not be surprised, therefore, that in each of these moments seeds of evil and war were being sown which have not yet all been reaped. Moreover—and this is critical for the Christian understanding of evil—the process is self-perpetuating. For each of these events, filled with evil sown in its past, is in turn a new seed which will sprout and be harvested in some future. And so the process goes on with no foreseeable end. Clearly, it would not be possible to give a full account of present international problems without, finally, tracing them back to the beginning of human history. It is precisely this fact, that we are in the grip of a past going all the way back to the very beginning, that is indicated by the Christian doctrine of the fall.

A similar sort of analysis of the historical character of evil could be given on the individual and personal level. In my home there are three children maturing into selfhood. Do they have a real chance to become persons not infected with anxiety, hatred, and guilt? Unfortunately, no. For they are growing up in a home with parents who, however much they seek to avoid this, frequently fail them. Instead of giving them security whenever they are anxious, their parents, themselves insecure, often explode in exasperation at the children's behavior. Instead of giving them acceptance and love whenever such is needed, their parents may be conversing with a friend and resent being disturbed, or be off to the office or a dinner party to which the child has no access. Accordingly, the children learn that they must fend for themselves, that they cannot fully trust even their parents, that life is often hard and cruel and unloving. And they may well resent this and become filled with unhappiness, bitterness, and hatred. Is it their fault if they then become self-centered, hateful persons? What else could they become in such a setting? Have they not been trapped into it at the very moments of their lives when they were young and tender and defenseless, when they bruised easily? Certainly they do not bear sole responsibility for the distortions in their personalities. But neither can their parents be held entirely responsible. For the parents themselves have become what they are— weak, inadequate, insecure, distrustful—because of the home situations in which they matured. And so on ad infinitum. Clearly, the evils in personal lives are handed on from generation to generation almost like a dread hereditary disease, though the transmission here is primarily social, not biological. To understand these evils there is no stopping with this generation or that; we must push all the way back to the beginnings if we are to have a full and adequate interpretation.

The Christian doctrine of the fall is the vivid expression of the fact that, however much human evil may have its present locus in our distorted selves and diseased communities, it has in a certain sense been foisted upon us by a history which we have not chosen but from which we cannot escape, a history going back to the beginning of the human species, to Adam.

## III.

It is in this corrupted history, according to the gospel, that God has acted in and through Jesus Christ to free humankind from bondage to sin and evil. What, now, was this action of God? Was it an action in which he laid down the proper laws of human conduct, for example, in the Sermon on the Mount? Was it an action through which he gave us an example, in Jesus of Nazareth, of how we ought to live? Was it an action in which he appeased his own wrath by sacrifice of his son? We cannot adequately understand the action of God in Jesus Christ simply by reciting such well-worn formulas as these. Only through seeing it in the context of the whole history reported in the Bible can we grasp what is involved.

There is not time to review the full movement of Old Testament history, but we must touch on a few high points. It is generally agreed by Old Testament scholars that the great turning point of Israel's history occurred probably during the thirteenth century, B.C., with the series of events that included the exodus from Egypt and the covenant with God at Mt. Sinai. For it was in and through these events that the Hebrews bound themselves to their God, and he to them. Yahweh would be their God; they would be his people. Throughout the invasion of Canaan, the wars with the Philistines, the long struggle with Canaanite baal religion, and finally the destruction of the two kingdoms and the exile, it was the memory of the covenant with Yahweh that provided a thread of continuity in terms of which the prophets and others could interpret the real meaning of what was happening to Israel.

The great creative writer, "J," known to us through the careful researches of modern historians, produced (around 950 B.C.) a history of Israel—the first great piece of historical writing anywhere and the nucleus of the Old Testament. In it he made two things especially clear: (a) That it was Yahweh, the God of the Hebrews, who created the world, and who continues to work toward the realization of his own purposes in the world; and (b) That this God, who is the source of all existence and who works in and through all of history, has acted in a special way in Hebrew history, making a covenant with Israel, the chosen agent of his purposes. In the light of J's important historical work the great prophets of the eighth century—Amos, Hosea, Micah, and Isaiah—found it possible to interpret contemporary historical events as also the expression of the purposes of God. The movements of Assyria against Israel and Judah, said Isaiah, are not due simply to the imperialistic designs of the Assyrian king. Rather they are instrumentalities of the judgment of Yahweh upon the Israelites who have failed to keep their side of the covenant.

> Ah, Assyria, the rod of my anger,
>   the staff of my fury!
> Against the godless nation I send him,
>   and against the people of my wrath I
>     command him . . . (Isa. 10:5, 6, RSV).

In the light of their awareness that in Israel's injustice, apostasy, and degeneracy the purposes of God were not being fulfilled, the prophets looked forward to a day in the future—the Day of the Lord (Amos 5:18-20; Isa. 2:12-22; 13:6-16; etc.)—when God's rule over all history would be fully manifest in destruction of his enemies, and his will would finally be done. All of history—past, present, future—was in the hands of God, and the course of history was moving inexorably toward the fulfillment of his purpose to establish perfectly his kingdom. However, because history had become the domain of sinful rebellion against God, it seemed clear this great event could happen only if God were to intervene directly, perhaps overturning the powers now loose in history (as men like Zephaniah, Zechariah, Joel, and others thought), perhaps through transforming the evil heart of man from "stone" into "flesh" (as Ezekiel declared), perhaps through entering into a "new covenant" with man (as Jeremiah hoped). But surely the kingdom of God, that great transformation and fulfillment of all history, will come, and then even

> The wolf shall dwell with the lamb,
>   and the leopard shall lie down with the kid,
> and the calf and the lion and the fatling together,
>   and a little child shall lead them.
> The cow and the bear shall feed;
>   their young shall lie down together;
>   and the lion shall eat straw like the ox.
> The sucking child shall play over the hole of the asp,
>   and the weaned child shall put his hand on the adder's den.

They shall not hurt or destroy
  in all my holy mountain;
for the earth shall be full of the knowledge of the Lord
  as the waters cover the sea (Isa. 11:6-9, RSV).

The Old Testament period moves forward toward its end in a rising crescendo of hope. The expectation of the mighty act of God which will transform everything into the fulfillment of his purposes is the dominant theme in the years immediately preceding the Christian era.

It is in this context of hope and expectation that the New Testament must be understood and the significance of Jesus Christ apprehended. For the New Testament writers were convinced that precisely this hope was fulfilled in Christ. The long historical preparation recorded in the Old Testament had finally borne fruit in the appearance of an itinerant preacher and healer, Jesus of Nazareth, and particularly in his death and resurrection. Jesus himself had come preaching that "the time is fulfilled, and the kingdom of God is at hand" (Mark 1:15); his powers of healing seemed to him and his disciples clear evidence that the kingdom was already in their midst (Luke 11:20; 17:21). Although Jesus' execution as a common criminal appeared to call into question the validity of this conviction, it was not long before they became convinced that God had raised him from the dead, fully vindicating his message and unequivocally designating him as the one who was to establish the kingdom among humans (cf. Rom. 1:4). The long expected New Age, then, was *now here,* and it was known to Jesus' followers! God's decisive action in history through which he was overthrowing the power of evil and sin was actually in process! The new covenant between God and man, which Jeremiah had expected, was now established, and people were being given the new hearts for which Ezekiel had hoped. The kingdom of God was here, and people were being called to live in it!

A scattered selection of passages, characteristic of the New Testament as a whole, underlines the point: "the kingdom of God has come upon you" (Mt. 12:28); "this is what was spoken by the prophet" (Acts 2:16); "he has delivered us from the dominion of darkness and transferred us to the kingdom of his beloved Son" (Col. 1:13); "if any one is in Christ, he is a new creation; the old has passed away, behold, the new has come" (2 Cor. 5:17); "you have been born anew, not of perishable seed but of imperishable" (1 Pet. 1:23); "the darkness is passing away and the true light is already shining . . . it is the last hour" (1 John 2:8, 18). Thus the long expected dramatic intervention of God in human history—the great Day of the Lord— had begun with Jesus' ministry, was certified with his resurrection, and was soon to be completed with his expected return on the clouds of heaven as the Son of Man. The earliest Christians were persons who knew themselves to be living "between the times"—between the *beginning* of the final transformation of all of history, and its *completion*.

The deepest significance of the New Testament for Christian ethics is not to be found in its moral teachings, nor in Jesus' example of good behavior, nor in some dogma about a divine transaction changing God's attitude toward us. It is to be found rather in its presentation of God's mighty act of sacrifice without reservation (Phil. 2) through which his faithful love and forgiveness of mankind became both visible and effective in human history, establishing the kingdom of God. As Paul puts it, "While we were yet sinners" and his "enemies we were reconciled to God by the death of his Son" (Rom. 5:8, 10). "In this the love of God was made manifest among us," says the writer of 1 John, "that God sent his only Son into the world, so that we might live through him" (4:9). This new awareness of the presence of God's love in their midst freed the first Christians of their doubts and fears. No longer had humans to live a self-centered existence, always building walls between themselves and others for protection against betrayals and hurts, for it was now clear that God—the very foundation of all existence—is absolutely trust-worthy; he never betrays. So a human, also, could take the risk of loving God and his fellows without reservation. Thus God's act of love, in making it possible for man to love, literally transformed him into a "new creation" (2 Cor. 5:17) no longer centered in himself but centered instead in God. And thus it became possible for human lives to manifest God's love, for human love to become the vehicle in history and society of the divine love.

From this brief resume of the biblical story, it should be clear that God's action in Christ was not an event isolated or separated from the rest of history. On the contrary, it was the moment in which God's activity in every moment of history came to sharp focus. The entire Old Testament is the story of God's loving preparation and education of a people—who originally thought of him as essentially a God of war and violence—so that they could apprehend him as one whose nature is love. Thus, from the creation until the appearance of Jesus Christ, God in his love was working with man, preparing the way, so that finally he could break into human history decisively as love. Again, the history of the church since Jesus Christ is the story of the spreading of this message and fact of God's love through all history to all people. Jesus Christ is the center, the focal point of history, through which has been revealed the ultimate fact of history: that it rests in the will and purposes of a loving God. In this sense Jesus Christ is the supreme act of God. It is to this action, through which the divine love flows into human history and becomes a fact within history, that we are called to respond.

## IV.

If the history reported in the Bible be accepted as revealing the nature and purposes of the ultimate reality with which we have to do—and Christian faith makes just this affirmation—then the moral context in which we live and act is not defined exclusively by the corrupted sinful history in which we are living. On the contrary, the most significant reality which we confront is not human sin but the God who acts to redeem us from that sin. Whereas the analysis of human sinfulness taken by itself might lead us to despair of any possibility for real community among people, the revelation that God himself, creator of the heavens and the earth, is working in love to extricate man from his plight, restores hope for humankind and for human history. For "if God be for us, who can be against us?" (Rom. 8:31, KJV). Doubtless sin and rebellion are still with us, but now we know that this empirical state of human existence is not the last word.

It is necessary to sketch out a bit further the implications of this fact for ethics. Right action must now be understood in relation to God's redemptive activity: What is the proper response to the God who loves? The answer is given in summary in the first letter of John and in words of Jesus: "Beloved, if God so loved us, we also ought to love one another" (1 John 4:11). "You shall love the Lord your God with all your heart . . . [and] you shall love your neighbor as yourself" (Mk. 12:30, 31). We must give ourselves in service to our neighbors, as God sacrifices himself for us. The radical demands this obligation lays upon us we will consider in later chapters. For now we must see certain broader implications of the fact that our love is called forth by God's love.

In the first place, it must be emphasized that our love is in *response* to God's love. As we noted earlier, man's problem is precisely that he is imprisoned within walls of distrust, fear, self-interest, and guilt. Therefore, he neither really desires, nor is he able, freely to give himself in love to neighbor and enemy. Only as God frees us to love, by giving himself to us in love and sustaining us for love, are we enabled to act out of the conviction that the ultimate reality with which we have to do is love. As we are freed from fears about our own security and enabled to trust that he who created us will sustain and forgive us, it becomes possible for us to love and serve others with a new spontaneity and creativity. It even begins to be possible to love those who hate and distrust us; we come to know ourselves as called to lives of reconciling and redemptive action among our fellows. For to be truly responsive to God's action, our activity must be modeled after God's own act in Jesus Christ, in which "while we were [still his] enemies we were reconciled to God by the death of his Son" (Rom. 5:10). We must, therefore, devote ourselves to restoring the broken community among people if we would respond to God the Reconciler.

In the second place, we must remember that the one who reconciles us to himself in Jesus Christ is none other than our Creator and the Creator of all that exists. Our response to God, then, cannot be in relation only to God's reconciling activity; we must also be responsive to him as Creator, the one who out of his love has brought the world into being. A loving response here begins with acknowledgment of the goodness of existence as God has made it. We must not begrudge being just the persons he has made us, nor the place in time and space where he has set us; we must willingly take our part in the created order, rejoicing in the goodness of God's world. We must love that world, seeking to know it better, so that we can more readily find our proper place in it. The artist's search for and appreciation of the beauty in God's creation, and the scientist's and scholar's search for truth about the universe, are indispensable dimensions of man's proper response to the goodness of the created order. Schweitzer has popularized the conviction that we should express "reverence for life"; if we would truly respond to God as Creator, we must have reverence for all of creation, reverence for being.[1]

Finally, we must say that for the Christian faith he who has brought us into being and has revealed himself as reconciling love is also continuously present to all his creation, working out his purposes in it and revealing himself to it. If we are to respond to God, we must also respond to him as Holy Spirit, present in every event of history, providentially ordering it according to his loving purposes. This requires us to look for God's hand in everything that happens to us. We will see his blessings in those things which seem to us undeserved goods. In those events which frustrate us, we will see his love judging and restraining our sinful ways. In the struggles of our social existence—e.g., the tensions between the United States and Russia on the international scene—as well as in our personal affairs, we will always seek to respond to God's providential ordering of the course of history. In every happening it is God's loving hand which we must discern and to which we must respond, for the God of Christian faith is also the Holy Spirit, living and active in every moment.

Our response to the God who loves must be characterized then by all three of these dimensions: response to him as Redeemer and Reconciler, as Creator, and as living, governing Spirit. For it is the one trinitarian God whose love has come to us in Jesus Christ.

We can now see that the Christian moral life cannot be simply a life of imitation of Jesus nor a life guided by some eternal principles supposedly embodied in the Ten Commandments or in Jesus' teachings. For it is a life most fundamentally defined by its context and source: God's action—a reality first apprehended in our dawning awareness of his act in Jesus Christ, but continuously present with us in every moment. And it finds its fulfillment in our free response, new and creative in every moment, searching for his will for that moment. Christian faith—faith in the God who reveals himself in Jesus Christ—is the presupposition of the Christian moral life; the Christian life is the product and outworking of Christian faith. Christian ethics is the attempt to understand and interpret this continuous dialogue between God's action and our response.

[1]Cf. H. Richard Niebuhr *Radical Monotheism and Western Culture* (New York: Harper, 1960), pp. 31-37.

# Chapter 4

# The Church and the World*

Right action, from the perspective of Christian faith, begins not with humanity's aspirations and desires but with God's act in Jesus Christ. People's desires and aims gain their character from the historical situation in which they emerge, but human history itself—and therefore the communities that arise within it—has become distorted and confused and the bearer of evil powers of distrust and hatred. These powers in turn perpetuate themselves through shaping the character of the persons and communities which emerge within the context of history, and transmitting that history to future generations. Thus man's situation is a vicious one from which he cannot extricate himself. But the claim of the Christian gospel is that God, out of his unfailing mercy and gracious love, has broken through the shell of unfaith and lovelessness by himself coming in the person of Jesus Christ, bringing forgiveness and reconciliation, healing the wounds of estrangement among people and between humankind and God. Right action therefore begins with appropriate response to God's action of love. The good life is nothing else than the life of love and self-giving elicited from us as we become aware of God's loving sacrifice for us. To live in response to God is thus to become a channel to our fellow human beings of the same love and self-giving with which God came to us; it is, in short, to become "ambassadors for Christ" through whom God's reconciling love makes its appeal to our fellows. "He who loves is born of God and knows God. He who does not love does not know God; for God is love" (1 John 4:7, 8).

What, now, is this love that is at once required and made possible

---

*From *The Context of Decision* (New York: Abingdon Press, 1961), pp. 48-70.

by God's act of condescension and self-giving in Christ? There is no question that for the Christian faith the ultimate model or picture in terms of which Christian love must be understood is God's own act of self-giving through coming to humankind in history and ultimately, despite man's rejection, reconciling humanity to himself. "In this is love," says the first letter of John, "not that we loved God but that he loved us" (4:10). Here, then, is the final norm of Christian ethics in terms of which all else must be understood. But this model, this picture, this norm, may itself, when interpreted as the standard in terms of which I am to order my conduct, seem abstract and irrelevant and almost unreal.

## I.

God loves me, we say, and I should love my neighbor in response— but what does this really tell me about how I should govern the details of my life? What, after all, does this tell me about the vocation I should choose, or whom I should marry, or whether I should buy a new car this year? The decisions I have to make from day to day are small and concrete. How does the bare fact of the Christian claim that God loves me, forgives me, reconciles me to himself, affect these decisions? The fact that many different and even contradictory ways of understanding the Christian's situation in society have appeared in Christian history is evidence enough that the implications of God's love for concrete behavior are by no means clear and unambiguous.

Radical Christian groups such as the Reformation Anabaptists have always insisted that the right interpretation of these implications is to be found in the teachings of Jesus. Here is set forth in the most radical form what God's love requires in our relations with our fellows, and this picture is fully consistent with the self-giving, self-sacrificial, reconciling love of God which is proclaimed in the Christian gospel. If Christians have been all too willing to say that Jesus' ethic is an ethic that applies to God's coming kingdom but not to this present world, or is appropriate for monks but not for the great mass of ordinary Christians, or applies to personal life but not the social order, or if they have otherwise "watered down" the terrible implications of Jesus' understanding of God's will, it is only because they have felt that the burden here laid on us is more than we can bear. That is, they have tended to answer the question of how we ought to respond to God in terms of their own notions of human possibilities, rather than simply by reference to God's revelation of himself and the radicalness of his love. But we dare not thus begin with man: we must rather begin by accepting the authority of God's revelation to reshape our every conception of human possibility. We must, then, take very seriously the claim of the Anabaptist-Mennonite tradition that the radical sayings of Jesus set before us a clear picture of the ethical import of God's act, and that here is portrayed precisely the kind of conduct required in our relations with our fellows.

What, now, was Jesus' teaching regarding our relations to others? We have not time here, nor is it necessary, to analyze his teachings in detail. It is well known that Jesus' activity centered in the conviction that the kingdom of God was coming, indeed, was already present in his ministry. All of Jesus' teaching and action were governed by this expectation and awareness of the presence of the kingdom. And this fact, in turn, rendered every other consideration irrelevant. "No one can serve two masters" (Matt. 6:24), so it was necessary to distinguish very clearly between all human interests and values and God's demands. Even the basic needs of life were unimportant in the face of the demand to participate in the kingdom.

> Therefore do not be anxious, saying, "What shall we eat?" or "What shall we drink?" or "What shall we wear?" For the Gentiles seek all these things; and your heavenly Father knows that you need them all. But seek first his kingdom and his righteousness . . . (Matt. 6:31-33, RSV).

Indeed, one must be willing to give up anything and everything for the kingdom of God.

> The kingdom of heaven is like treasure hidden in a field, which a man found and covered up; then in his joy he goes and sells all that he has and buys that field. Again, the kingdom of heaven is like a merchant in search of fine pearls, who, on finding one pearl of great value, went and sold all that he had and bought it (Matt. 13:44, 45, RSV).

It is not enough merely to give up material blessings of this life for the kingdom; we must even be ready to sacrifice our own bodies if they stand in the way of obedience.

> If your hand causes you to sin, cut it off; it is better for you to enter life maimed than with two hands to go to hell. . . . And if your foot causes you to sin, cut it off; it is better for you to enter life lame than with two feet to be thrown into hell. And if your eye causes you to sin, pluck it out; it is better for you to enter the kingdom of God with one eye than with two eyes to be thrown into hell (Mark 9:43-47, RSV).

Thus the demand laid upon us is absolute. We must be willing to give up any and every tie to human values and goods for God's kingdom. The first requirement laid on man is to decide, to say *no* to self and to everything that belongs to the self, and to say *yes* to God's demands, however radical or impossible they may appear to be.

The radicalness of these demands comes out most clearly, perhaps, in the great series of antitheses found in the fifth chapter of Matthew. Jesus is here portrayed as rejecting certain of the basic commandments of the Jewish Torah. We must remember that the Torah, as interpreted by the Pharisees and others of Jesus' time, was understood as prescribing the kind of behavior appropriate in every conceivable situation. The complex legalistic interpretations did not grow out of some perverse obtuseness of Jews trying to obscure God's will; on the contrary, it grew out of their conscientious efforts to discover and apply God's will for every situation in which a first-century Jew might find himself. In view of this, it is important for us to note that Jesus rejects the Torah as thus interpreted, not because it is made to cover every aspect of life, i.e., not because it is too strict, but rather because it is *not strict enough,* not far-reaching enough in its penetration into all aspects of human existence (cf. Matt. 23:23). Listen to Jesus' words:

> You have heard that it was said to the men of old, "You shall not kill; and whoever kills shall be liable to judgment." But I say to you that every one who is angry with his brother shall be liable to judgment; whoever insults his brother shall be liable to the council, and whoever says, "You fool!" shall be liable to the hell of fire. . . .
>
> You have heard that it was said, "You shall not commit adultery." But I say to you that every one who looks at a woman lustfully has already committed adultery with her in his heart. . . .
>
> You have heard that it was said, "An eye for an eye and a tooth for a tooth." But I say to you, Do not resist one who is evil. But if any one strikes you on the right cheek, turn to him the other also; and if any one would sue you and take your coat, let him have your cloak as well; and if any one forces you to go one mile, go with him two miles. Give to him who begs from you, and do not refuse him who would borrow from you.
>
> You have heard that it was said, "You shall love your neighbor and hate your enemy." But I say to you, Love your enemies and pray for those who persecute you, so that you may be sons of your Father who is in heaven; for he makes his sun rise on the evil and on the good, and sends rain on the just and on the unjust (Matt. 5:21-22, 27, 28, 38-45, RSV).
>
> If you love those who love you, what credit is that to you? For even sinners love those who love them. And if you do good to those who do good to you, what credit is that to you? For even sinners do the same. And if you lend to those from whom you hope to receive, what credit is that to you? Even sinners lend to sinners, to receive as much again. But love your enemies, and do good, and lend, expecting nothing in return; and your reward will be great, and you will be sons of the Most High; for he is kind to the ungrateful and the selfish (Luke 6:32-35, RSV).

The thing for us to note here is the absoluteness, indeed the *impossibleness,* of Jesus' demands. The old law had held murder to be wrong. Jesus does not challenge that judgment. But to think that working out elaborate legal definitions of murder and then staying within the letter of the law is to fulfill God's will is simply foolishness. It is not the murderer alone who transgresses God's command; anyone who feels and expresses anger "shall be liable to judgment." Or take the matter of adultery. The mere presence of illicit sexual desire, however unexpressed, however deeply hidden in the heart, is violation of God's holy will. And what of our relations to our enemies, to those whom we dislike and who mistreat us? Toleration is the very most that can rightly be expected here, we might well think; if we do not repay them with the coin they give us, surely no more is required. But no! Jesus insists we should *love* our enemies, we should do positive good to those who harm us, we should give aid and comfort to those who would destroy us. It is not enough that we refrain from violation of the law—even Jesus' stringent interpretations of the laws regarding murder and adultery—however impossible that might seem; it is not enough that our relations with friends and loved ones be characterized by perfect love; it is not enough that we tolerate our enemies, however difficult that might be: we are to love perfectly, not simply those who love us, but those who hate us! A more extreme demand than this could scarcely be imagined. A demand more impossible of fulfillment could hardly be laid upon us who find it difficult even to love our friends.

But, after all, God makes his sun to shine and his rain to fall on good and evil alike; he shows no partiality to those who love and obey him. He loves all and blesses all. Those who do not know the love of God might have some excuse for not loving their enemies. But Jesus' disciples, knowing God's love and forgiveness of the lowliest and most rebellious of sinners seeking to destroy his kingdom, have no excuse for treating their enemies otherwise than with a similar love. "You, therefore," as Matthew sums it up, "must be perfect, as your heavenly Father is perfect" (5:48).

## II.

Jesus' ethic is the ethic of the kingdom of God. As such, it is a description of the character of the community which is ruled by God's love and through which God's love becomes empirical reality shaping the actual interpersonal relations of human beings here on earth. It is important to note this is an ethic for the church militant, not simply for the church triumphant. It is taken for granted that those to whom Jesus is speaking are in a situation not favorable to their existence or their views: they must deal with "enemies," but they are to "love" them. Indeed, it is precisely in this loving of the enemies (of themselves and even of God) that they become "sons" of God (Luke 6:35; Matt. 5:44-45; cf. 1 John 4), i.e., living members of his household and kingdom, who are vehicles of God's love in human history. The community of reconciliation to which Jesus' followers belong is thus the cutting edge of God's love bringing redemption to rebellious people in sinful human history (2 Cor. 5:19-20).

The radical demands of Jesus' ethical teachings are obviously consistent with the fundamental claim of the Christian gospel, that in Jesus Christ God himself really has broken and is breaking into human history, transforming humanity's sinful existence with his redemptive love. If there were no actual community of living people in which the wounds of distrust, unfaithfulness, and hatred were in fact being healed through forgiveness and reconciling love, it is hard to see how the gospel of God's love could be anything more than an abstract and empty pronouncement—a far cry from the "good news" of the real transformative power of God's love in human lives proclaimed by the earliest Christians. Jesus' ethical teachings express in the most concrete terms the way in which God's love becomes an actual fact in the lives of men and women. It becomes an empirical historical reality as and when human beings forgive and become reconciled with their enemies, not in the sense of some pious, martyred turning of the other cheek, but so that the enemy knows he has met in this person the very love of God. Those of us to whom God's love has been made known through the death of his Son are commanded to love our enemies so that they, too, can say with us and with Paul, "While we were enemies we were reconciled" (Rom. 5:10).

We can now see what the church is and must be for the perspective of Christian faith. It is nothing else than the community of reconciliation through which God's love is penetrating human history. It is the historical community in which God's love is known as real, and which therefore manifests forgiving and reconciling love toward its own historical enemies. It is the point within sinful and warring human history where the disloyalty and faithlessness characteristic of human affairs is actually being overcome by faith and hope and love. Christian faith believes that this church—at the front line of battle being waged within God's kingdom by rebels against his love—will ultimately take up within herself the world now in rebellion against God; thus her destiny is finally to become God's perfect kingdom. But at present the church is in no position to make any such claims to perfection or completeness. Although the church knows in the present—and this is the very presence of Christ's spirit within her—"a foretaste of the future" (Rom. 8:23, Goodspeed), her life here and now is one of suffering and inner struggle as she waits "for the sons of God to be disclosed" and for her own members "to be declared God's sons" (Rom. 8:19, 23, Goodspeed). The church must ever live then, oriented toward the future, toward this expected fulfillment. Her present existence falls within the early stages of the great transformation, but these do not have their real meaning unless and until their completion is realized (cf. Phil. 3:12-14). This is why Paul can deny the present fulfillment of the church's life and mission to the point of saying, finally, that it is in "hope we were saved" (Rom. 8:24).

### III.

We cannot here work out a full doctrine of the church, however important that might be to a fully developed Christian ethic. We can only sketch some of the implications for Christian ethics of the historical and theological fact of the church's reality. The church's significance for ethics derives from the fact that she is at the front lines of God's transforming of human existence through his redemptive love. Indeed, we might say the church is the very process of that transformation; she is the world being transformed. This means that the church can never separate herself from the world and remain the church. For the church's very reality lies in her being the point where God's love is overcoming man's rebellion.

> Once you were no people but now you are God's people; once you had not received mercy but now you have received mercy.... You are a chosen race, a royal priesthood, a holy nation, God's own people, *that you may declare the wonderful deeds* of him who called you out of darkness into his marvelous light (1 Pet. 2:10, 9, RSV, italics mine).

For the church to attempt to separate herself from humankind's rebellion through separating herself from rebellious people would be to dissolve her own reality. She would destroy herself externally through forsaking her true task, the overcoming of humankind's rebellion wherever found; and she would destroy herself internally by her supposition, incompatible with Christian humility, that sin and uncleanness reside principally in those from whom she has departed and not within her own members. But "if we say we have no sin, we deceive ourselves, and the truth is not in us. If we confess our sins, he is faithful and just, and will forgive our sins and cleanse us from all unrighteousness" (1 John 1:8, 9). The church is never in a position to make claims for herself, least of all, claims of her own sinlessness or perfection, for her very being lies in the acknowledgment that we are saved through the power of *God's* love, not through something that we ourselves are or might become. "We have this treasure in earthen vessels, to show that the transcendent power belongs to God and not to us" (2 Cor. 4:7).

The church, then, the community in which God's love is known to be real, can never afford to separate herself from the world, for her mission to the world is of her very essence. This is the basis of the missionary and evangelistic impulse without which a community cannot be Christian.[1] It is not at all clear, however, that our usual missionary efforts—sending a few people to "foreign lands" or "heathen peoples" while the church at home remains a stable community with no real outreach to her own environment—are much more than a way of avoiding the demand to be an effective mission in the world.

The fact that the church is the process of transformation of the world means that no sharp distinction between church and world can be sustained. A process of change always participates in both realities, that *from* which the change is occurring and that *toward* which it is moving. A naturalized citizen does not immediately give up everything from the old country and take on all the customs of the new, and it is always impossible to draw a sharp line setting off those who have decisively taken up the new way of life from those who have retained the old. We may well be "free citizens of Heaven" (Phil. 3:20, Weymouth), but we still live on earth and we await the final transformation in which our citizenship will be realized. The terms "church" and "world," therefore, do not stand so much for static realities posed over against each other, each sharply definable, as for terminals in the living process of history in which we exist. "World" refers to that condition of sin and rebellion from which we are being changed through God's love; "church" refers to that community of love into which we are being moved. In this sense the church really exists only eschatologically, as the goal of history, the realization of the kingdom of God, that which is to come when God's purposes are finally and fully realized, that for which we hope and pray and for which we live.

Without this hope and expectation and confidence that God is actually changing this world into his kingdom of love, it would be meaningless and absurd for us to give our lives in absolute self-sacrifice and love. Within the context of this hope, however, such self-giving makes sense, for then it can be seen as the very process through which the transformation of human existence is coming about. The actual churches in which we live are in the world, and the world is in them as well, and therefore no clear line between church and world can be drawn. But the eschatological church, which is taking up the world into herself and transforming it into the community of the love of God, is also present in our actual churches, and through them in the world, and it is for this reality which is to come—a "foretaste" being already present—that we live and move and have our being as persons who love others in response to God's love.

## IV.

What, now, has all this to do with the concrete problems of right and wrong, with the decisions we must make daily? We have been describing in theological terms the *context* of the Christian life, the situation in which all decisions and actions occur and which should be present to our minds whenever we act. There are three essential factors in this context, none of which can be ignored. The first, of course, is God's act. Christian action must always be response to the gospel, a response of gratitude to God for his love. It should be clear by now that this act of God's love is not something concentrated exclusively on a particular point in past time, the appearance of Jesus of Nazareth in history. Although it is true that in a decisive way God's love broke into human history with Jesus Christ, it is necessary to go on and say that this was but a crucial beginning point of the process intended to culminate in the final establishment of God's kingdom of love among all people. God's act of love first becomes incarnate in human history with Jesus Christ, but it does not end there; it continues to work in and through human history until the end, when it reaches its completion. It is a historical act and thus takes time, as all historical acts do, but it is a historical act that ultimately will take up all of history into itself. God's act in Christ will not be completed, therefore, until the end of history has come.

This means that we in human history are living "between the times"—between the appearance of Christ and the end of the world, between the historical beginning of God's mighty act of salvation and its completion. We live in the period of transformation, the period in which God's love is an active force in human history: we live in the time of the church. For the Christian community, all decisions and actions must be governed by this consciousness that God has begun his great act of love, is even now acting, and shall finally establish his kingdom. This is the ultimate cosmic fact, the real truth about the universe and about history in terms of which all else must be judged. We are not to take our bearings simply from the empirical historical situation in which we find ourselves. Not even the ideals, ideas, values, and goals which we can discern in our situation are to be the basis in terms of which we orient our lives. Instead our lives must be oriented toward the past—God's historical act of self-giving in Jesus Christ, and the future—his final establishment of a community of love. For Christian ethics right and wrong cannot be decided merely in terms of the present situation in history, however impregnated with ideals our situation may appear to be. For the Christian ethic is historical-eschatological: it takes its bearings, not from what seems real and obvious in the present, but from the living past and the hoped for future.

Moreover, the Christian ethic, eschatological to the core, makes sense only from a point of view which does not judge things in terms of the possibilities or probabilities of the present but believes rather in God's ultimate triumph. It is this expectation that enables the Christian ethic to express itself in radical nonresistance. We saw before that in Jesus' teaching unequivocal love of enemies is required; indeed, it is in such self-giving that God's love becomes historically concrete. But self-sacrifice to enemies is both absurd and imprudent in any but an eschatological perspective. There is no reason to suppose that in history—in your life and mine—such love will always, or even usually, result in the transformation of enemies into friends. In its most notable exemplification it resulted in crucifixion. On any short-term view it should be obvious that power, not love, rules human history, that those who love and give themselves are only destroyed. "Pragmatic pacifism" is thus nonsense. But the Christian ethic is not rooted in any short-term judgments of this sort. It is rooted in an eschatological perspective in which the ultimate overcoming of the world by the power of God's love is expected. From this perspective, absolute self-giving makes sense. For faith, believing that God's purpose will prevail, it is possible, indeed only reasonable, to express that purpose through love, even though this means historical destruction. But this is true only for a faith that lives in this hope, not for any other perspective.

Thus, when we say that Christian ethics is founded in faith in God's act, we are making a most radical kind of statement with the most radical kind of consequences. It means very literally that "we look not to the things that are [or can be] seen [in this our present life] but to the things that are unseen; for the things that are seen are transient, but the things that are unseen are eternal" (2 Cor. 4:18). Right and wrong are not to be defined in terms of any utilitarian consequences, any human ideals or aspirations, any human desires or needs. They are to be defined only in terms of God's will and God's act of love even to enemies, in the confidence that finally God's purpose will prevail.

The context in which we act, however, is not exhaustively described simply by referring thus to God's act. God's purpose is for history and his act is in history as the presence of the historical community called the church. The actual situation and struggles of the church in and with the world are therefore the sociological dimensions of the context. There is no such thing as an individual Christian responding to God's act in isolation. The call to Christian faith always comes through the historical activity of the church; the love of God is always mediated to us through the actual love of other persons—parents, children, friends, teachers; our faith comes to us through the work of the church in history. Nor is it possible to respond to God's love in isolated individuality. For to respond to God's love is to serve our fellows with love, to become the vehicle through which God's love flows to them. God's love thus always comes to us through human community and it necessarily leads us back into human community. The church, we have seen, is just that community whose special historical mission is to witness to God's love and to be the channel through which that love flows into the world. Thus, response to God's love means entering into the church and its task of being the mediator of love to the world. There is no such thing as a Christian solitary: a Christian is inevitably involved in the work of the church.

## V.

We have thus far been discussing the nature of the church as though it were perfectly obvious just what historical community we were attempting to describe. But this is not the case. There are numerous communities claiming to be *the* church or a church. They have different, and even contradictory, conceptions and interpretations of their nature and mission. To what, then, are we actually referring when we speak of the church? We cannot here give a full theological description of the marks of the church, but at least this much must be said. It is necessary to be clear in our minds whether we are speaking *eschatologically* or *empirically* about the church. (This distinction is more appropriate theologically than what is sometimes called, in Platonic terms, the distinction between the "invisible" and "visible" church.) If we are speaking eschatologically of the church, the church is all mankind transformed into God's kingdom. Though the eschatological church is not now visible to our eyes, it is in the hope and expectation that God is working in history toward this end—however problematic this may appear from within history— that is at the heart of Christian faith. All of the forces of history are finally, in God's providence, being directed toward this end, though this can be seen only by God himself and believed only by faith; to the eye of the "natural man" the historical evidence hardly appears to warrant such high hope.

There is a community within history, however, which lives by just this hope. That community is the empirical church which knows herself, in faith, to have as her ultimate destiny nothing less than becoming God's perfect community of love. The empirical church thus consists of those who consciously and conscientiously live in response to God's act in Jesus Christ and in expectation of his ultimate transformation of all of human history. It is difficult to see, from this point of view, how the empirical church can be anything but a confessional "believers' church." In this, also, the Anabaptist "sectarians" appear to have been correct. There may be a sense in which all people are in the church, as the "church-type" churches[2] have maintained, and have symbolized through infant baptism. But if so, this becomes a reality only in the eschaton; it is not an empirical reality in our present historical existence as the church-type churches have in effect claimed. The actual historical community, through which God's love in Jesus Christ is mediated to the world, is that community of believers who have been seized by that love and in turn seek to respond to it through giving themselves as fully as they can in service to both neighbor and enemy.[3]

If the empirical church—the actual historical community through which God's love is moving into the "world"—is a believers' church, then we must take seriously certain implications. In the first place, it will be necessary for the church to realize that she is the *empirical,* not the eschatological, church (except by anticipation). That is, she is a church very much involved in the struggle to overcome the world and in consequence a church in which her relations to the world are always ambiguous. She can never claim to render judgment with God's mind; she can only claim to be a community of humble believers living by God's forgiveness and love. She must always recognize, therefore, that her judgments are *human* judgments, and as such are infected with shortsightedness and relativity, to say nothing of pride and sin. Even, nay especially! her judgments of her own nature and mission are of that character. She lives by the *hope* of becoming, in the eschaton, the true expression of God's will, but she knows that she is still engaged in the battle with the world at every point. She lives in her mission to bring God's love to the "world," but she recognizes that her judgment even about who or what is the "world" is finite and full of error. The empirical church must always seek out what she can call the "world" and there bring her ministrations of love and service, but she must reckon with her own limitations in making all of these judgments.

This means that the empirical church will realize that she defines herself, and the world over against her where she must work, largely in pragmatic terms. The church defines her own membership pragmatically, i.e. she includes within that membership all who appear in her judgment to be confessing the same Lord Jesus Christ and to be responding to his love with love to their fellows, all, in short, who, because they recognize their common faith and life, find they can work together as a community. In terms of this pragmatic definition the church of course must exercise discipline, excluding from her membership those who, because of their different understanding of God's love and of the church's work, find they cannot cooperate actively in her program but serve rather to obstruct or block her work. This matter of discipline is of course very difficult, for how does one exclude persons out of love for them? And yet, when it is remembered that all acts of the empirical church are pragmatic acts with no claims to final or ultimate justification, but simply the best human judgment to which the community can come in the light of its own understanding of its work in the world, the harsh and brittle edge so often apparent in church discipline will perhaps be somewhat tempered. If the empirical church claimed to be the eschatological community, and her binding and loosing here on earth were believed valid for heaven above and all eternity (cf. Matt. 16:19; 18:18), then it would be a different matter. But as long as the church remembers her empirical character and recognizes her own judgments as pragmatic and relative, she will realize there are other communities on earth through which God is also working, however difficult it may be for us to discern his work in those that differ radically from our understanding of the church's nature and mission. And it may well be that those whom our church finds she must exclude to carry on her work will find their proper task in God's kingdom within some other historical community.

It should be clear from this that just as the church's self-definition is pragmatic, so is her conception of "the world." For the conception of the world is relative to and polar with the conception of the church. The world is nothing but that place to which the church has been called to minister with God's love. The world consists of those who, as the empirical church sees it, are not yet consciously responding to God's gift in Jesus Christ and to whom, therefore, the church must witness. The world consists of those who, from the empirical church's vantage point, are not yet clear vehicles of God's forgiveness and redemption, and whom, therefore, the church must love and serve and forgive. In short, the world is nothing else than that place of real human need, as the empirical church sees it, to which the church finds she must give herself in response to God's love given for her need.

The conception of the world arises, then, because as the church proceeds in her work she finds some whose viewpoint and understanding, judgments and actions, seem so strange that she cannot effectively cooperate with them in bringing God's love and forgiveness to humans. Perhaps these others with these strange ways call themselves Russian Communists, or Roman Catholics, or Southern Baptists, or Rotarians—their name matters not. Whoever they are, they are those with whom, in our limitations, we find we cannot effectively do what we understand to be our God-given task; indeed, we may find it necessary to oppose them vigorously. For us they are the "world," pragmatically defined in terms of the concrete action which love seems to us to require. Whenever we think this distinction between church and world, between "us" and "them," is more than pragmatic, and that we are somehow *better* than they, we are no longer acknowledging that we live simply by God's gracious forgiveness. On the contrary, we are boasting of our own virtue and thereby become, in our spiritual pride, worse than they.

Despite all the difficulties in the distinction between church and world, it is one which we must make, for God's love is always mediated to us through some empirical community, and we in turn cannot respond to that love without taking up our task of service within some empirical community. To be human is therefore to live and work in terms of some such distinctions. Let us be careful not to confuse these empirical distinctions with those final distinctions holding for the eschaton; these God alone can make. The wheat cannot with certainty be distinguished from the tares until the time of the harvest (Matt. 13:24-30).

## VI.

We can now briefly tie together the various strands of this chapter. We have seen that the church is that community which remembers

Jesus Christ and expects the coming kingdom of God; or, to say the same thing in another way, which lives in conscious response to God's purpose which—all historical evidence to the contrary notwithstanding—will ultimately prevail. At the same time, precisely because the church recognizes that the eschaton has not yet come and that she lives in the midst of the relativities of history, the church knows herself as empirical and limited with her conceptions and decisions pragmatically shaped. She knows, therefore, that she must exercise discipline, but she knows also that her judgments cannot be final. She knows that she must seek out the needs of the world and there serve, but she knows that her understanding of the world is limited and inadequate. The empirical church is thus the effective sociological unit within which Christian decisions and actions occur. The polar realities of church and world constitute the actual sociological context (theologically defined) within which Christian deciding, purposing, acting, and working proceed from day to day and year to year. Hence, only through analyzing and interpreting the empirical situation in terms of this concept of church-and-world, will our political, economic, social, and other decisions and work be seen in their theological import, i.e., in terms of the relevance to them of the redemption of human history by God's love.

---

[1] It should be noted in passing that early Anabaptism was a missionary movement in just this sense—perhaps the first modern missionary movement—attempting to spread the love of God everywhere. See, e.g., F. H. Littell, "The Anabaptist Theology of Missions," *Mennonite Quarterly Review* (1947), 21:5-17. S. F. Pannabecker, "Missions, Foreign Mennonite," *Mennonite Encyclopedia* (Scottdale, Pa.: Mennonite Publishing House, 1955-59), 3.712-17.

[2] For the classical statement of the distinction between "church" and "sect" see Ernst Troeltsch, *The Social Teaching of the Christian Churches*. Trans. Olive Wyon (London: Allen & Unwin, 1931), esp. Vol. II.

[3] It might be well to observe here that in the light of this stringent "Anabaptist" view of the church, modern Mennonite churches—with their staid, bourgeois memberships, their comfortable adjustment to laissez-faire capitalist practices, their regular practice of baptizing the young when they complete catechism class whether they have mature Christian convictions or not, their unwillingness to practice any kind of significant church discipline—are very little different in actuality from Christian groups of the "church-type" tradition.

# Part Two:

# NONRESISTANCE AND ITS PROBLEMS

# Chapter 5

# Nonresistance and Responsibility*

### I.

Modern Christian pacifists and nonpacifists seem to hold in common at least one assumption about Christian ethics: that an ethic founded in nonresistant love leads inevitably to withdrawal from and failure to take responsibility for the social order, and, conversely, that an ethic which concerns itself with the exigencies of the social order must in some way compromise or even give up nonresistant love as its sole ethical norm and imperative. Beginning from this assumption, the "Christian realism" of a man like Reinhold Niebuhr insists that love is an "impossible possibility" for a man as a participant in the realities of social life, and that the best that can be hoped for in this age is some approximation to "justice" gained through and supported by the power of the state. The Christian as well as the non-Christian ought to help achieve and maintain such justice, even though to do so requires, as Niebuhr is convinced, that he forsake the Christian ideal of absolute nonresistance.[1] Starting from the same assumption, contemporary advocates of the historic Mennonite strategy of withdrawal from the responsibilities of the sociopolitical order, insist anew that the serious Christian disciple, whose basic motivation and objective is nonresistant love, cannot participate in the power struggles of a non-Christian world.[2] A tacit admission of the same dichotomy is present in the widespread liberal-pacifist interpretation of the political relevance of Christian ethics in terms of the watered down notion of "nonviolent resistance" instead of the more radical

*From *Concern* No 6. A Pamphlet Series for Questions of Christian Renewal (Scottdale, Pa.: Herald Press, 1958)

and difficult notion of nonresistance. Though each of these positions differs sharply from the others, they all agree on the disparity, and even the contradiction, between the realities and necessities of the social order and radical nonresistance.

Acceptance of this dichotomy leaves theological ethics, as well as the acting Christian, in a very difficult position, for it implies that the basic orientation of Christian ethics removes it from concern with the deepest problems of society. One then must bypass the specifically Christian ethical consciousness, either through invoking Old Testament ethics (after the manner of Calvin) or "orders of creation" (after the manner of Brunner) or "natural law" (after the manner of the Thomists) as somehow level with or even taking precedence over the ethics of Jesus; or through showing that the radicalness of Jesus' ethic was a function of and essentially relevant only to his own eschatological expectations of the imminent end of the world (Schweitzer) and that therefore Jesus could ignore a problem which is nevertheless fundamental to our situation; or through insisting on the radical otherness of God's demands from man's—even redeemed man's—possibilities, an otherness so great that it is necessary to invoke principles and criteria for decision making which have no clearly Christian basis (Reinhold Niebuhr). Each of these positions involves the attempt to find some locus *outside* of the specifically Christian consciousness of the demand for nonresistant love, which locus can then serve as the basis for developing an ethic of society and can serve as a guide to the Christian in his life in the world. Needless to say, all such positions suffer the theological embarrassment of not being based clearly in the Christian revelation. It would seem, then, that one whose ethic is based on the revelation in Jesus Christ is forced by the apparent dichotomy between love and the social order to withdraw from the power struggles.

But such withdrawal proves to be theologically quite as embarrassing as attempted participation, for it leads to the negation of the very love in the name of which the withdrawal is made. If the nature of Christian love be understood in terms of the teaching of the Sermon on the Mount, on the one hand, and God's action of condescension, self-giving, and sacrifice unto death (Phil. 2:1-11), on the other, then love must always be understood as just that which never retreats from an evil situation, but always advances into it totally without regard for itself. The more evil is the situation, the more urgent is the demand on love to become involved redemptively. We Mennonites have interpreted the injunction to love our enemies far too simply and too negatively as meaning that we should avoid getting into fights with those who do not agree with us. But this quietist interpretation is more stoic than Christian. Love is not that which keeps out of trouble, a means of remaining above and secure from the conflicts of this world. Love is precisely that which goes into the very heart of an evil situation and attempts to rectify it. Relief programs in which we attempt to minister to the needs of the world in the midst of the evils of war and hate are not enough. However concerned we are and ought to be about physical and spiritual suffering, as Christians we know that the real evil in human affairs is not suffering but sin. It is in the midst of sinful situations that love must be found working, if it is love at all. And the more sinful the situation, the greater is the imperative that love enter it. Every pagan form of goodness attempts to avoid sin at all costs; Christian love on the contrary expresses itself precisely in its drive into the very heart of sin. The Christian, if there is a Christian, must be one who is the very friend of sinners (cf. Matt. 11:19; Luke 7:34).

Love, then, in sharp contrast with every other conception of goodness, is that which is concerned precisely to relate itself to its enemies, to sinners. Love is in fact not a "that" at all which can exist in and by itself; love exists only as a relationship, a relationship in which one person gives or sacrifices everything in himself, not for those who deserve such sacrifice nor for those who love him, but just for those who would destroy him. God's love for man is evident not in that God loved man because man loved God, but in that while man was in enmity and rebellion against God, God was actively reconciling man to himself (Rom. 5:10; 1 John 4:10, 19, and passim). The Christian is not simply called on to love those who love him and are members of the "beloved community"; even the publicans and the Gentiles do that (Matt. 5:46, 47). Insofar as the love (i.e. the dynamic self-sacrificial self-giving of the Christian disciple and the Christian community) is directed largely to members of that community, the community is little different from the communities of paganism. The life of the Christian disciple and the Christian community must consist in the constant attempt to give unselfishly to just those persons and communities and forces which seem most bent on destroying it. Christian love, as perfectly exemplified in God's act in Christ, sacrifices itself for and to sin; Christian love gives itself to its own enemies. This self-sacrifice and self-giving to the evils of the sinful situation is so radical and thorough and complete that St. Paul finds it necessary to say that in its perfect expression, Christ, "who knew no sin" was made "to be sin . . , so that in him we might become the righteousness of God" (2 Cor. 5:21).

Love goes to the very heart of the most sinful situations that it can find, and there it gives of itself without any reservation whatsoever. This is the absurdity of the Christian ethic; it is an ethic of radical imprudence. The Anabaptist-Mennonite tradition has always tried to interpret love in the radical sense of the New Testament, but in its tendency to withdraw from participation in the power struggles of the world it has badly compromised itself. On the Mennonite view, it is just in the power struggles, where self-centered and selfish individuals and groups attempt to dominate others and subject them, that are to be found both the essence and the most terrible expression of sin. For this reason Mennonites have felt unable to participate in these struggles. And yet, it is the character of love, not that it retreats from its opposite, but that it rushes in trying to act redemptively. Though certainly one cannot attempt to dominate others in the name of love, neither can one ever withdraw from sinful situations of attempted domination in the name of love. The tendency in the Anabaptist-Mennonite tradition has been to see clearly the first side of this paradox and to neglect the other side. And from this has followed the conviction that we have a right—nay, even a duty—to withdraw from certain aspects of human life and society simply because we think those aspects are sinful. But this is failing to love, just as certainly as is action out of the sinful desire to dominate. In sharp opposition to any strategy of withdrawal, which is always motivated by the kind of love known to the publicans and Gentiles, Christian love always takes responsibility for the sinful situation.[3]

The crucial question, then, is not whether as Christians we have some sort of responsibility for the social and political orders in which we live, but rather, what is the nature of that responsibility, and how must it express itself? It should be clear at the outset that this responsibility that we have for the society in which we live is not simply an outgrowth of or rationalization of the fact that we happen to belong to a certain group and a certain nation. Certainly we have obligations to these groups deriving from the fact that God has created us in and through a people who have given of themselves for us; and our response to his (and their) gifts to us should be one of gratitude and awareness of special obligations owed both to the Creator and to those through whom he brought us into being: the family, the community, the nation, etc. But our responsibility for the social order goes beyond the necessity to respond to the fact and nature of our creation. As Christians, our responsibility derives more directly and more decisively from God's action as Redeemer, from God's action in Jesus Christ. It is the obligation laid on us to love our brother as our proper response to God's prior love for us that is the basis for our concern for the social context in which our brother lives. Our responsibility for our brother in all aspects of his being derives from the necessity of our being responsive to God's love and mercy towards us. Conversely, it is not possible to respond to God's love or be obedient to his demand without taking responsibility for our brother. Responsibility for the brother and responsibility for the society of which he (as well as we) is a part thus derives directly from our responsibility to God. It is a religious responsibility from which no evasion of any kind is possible and it must be taken with absolute seriousness.

## II.

The responsibility laid upon us for our fellow human beings may be conveniently analyzed in terms of three aspects. The first is accepted in some form in all lines of the Christian tradition, and hence need not be developed in detail here. It may be described as our evangelistic or missionary responsibility: our responsibility to preach the gospel. God has given us the opportunity and laid upon us the obligation to witness to the truth of his revelation in Jesus Christ, to make him known to all people. Sometimes this task of witnessing has been interpreted in the narrow terms of simply speaking certain words or distributing tracts or something of the sort, but the Mennonite tradition has always known that this witness must be in the deepest sense a witness of the whole life. Our words no doubt must point to what God has done, but unless our lives have been transformed and themselves give witness to God's love, our words are empty. God's redemption is not merely an intellectual thing, but something that involves the totality of man's existence and being, and therefore it is with the totality of his being that man must speak of God's grace. The first aspect of our responsibility to our fellow humans is, then, so to live and speak that we witness to God's love for mankind. We must preach, we must freely and willingly do deeds of service and mercy, we must participate in a community in which the members truly love one another.

But simply witnessing to the truth as we see the truth does not exhaust the responsibilities of the Christian disciple toward his fellows. Witnessing is an expression of our love for our fellow, but love is more than simply witnessing. It is, in fact, possible to witness without love, as did Jonah, and as does anyone who points the finger of scorn and judgment on his neighbor or his society but does not so sympathize with the sufferings of that society as to participate in them himself. If the action of God in Christ is our model of love, it becomes clear that love is not something that stands afar off, as it were, and shouts a "witness" to those for whom it takes responsibility. This is in fact precisely the difference between the Old Testament and the New. In the former, God sent his word via his messengers, the prophets and others; in the latter, he himself came into human society to share in the grief and sin of human existence. Witnessing, taken by itself, can very easily become an attempt to do precisely the reverse of love, namely to manipulate others, to bring others to a change in belief and life in accordance with what we happen to think is right. The fanatic, the persecutor, the inquisitor of every age, are all witnesses to their faith, and in many cases they think it is Christian faith to which they are witnessing. Love does more than simply witness to its own convictions: love has real concern for the other as he actually is, not simply as I happen to think that he ought to be. As Brunner has put it: "To love a human being means to accept his existence, as it is given to me by God, and thus to love him *as he is*. For only if I love him thus, that is, as this particular sinful person, do I love *him*. For this is what he really is. Otherwise I love an idea—and in the last resort this means that I am merely loving myself."[4]

This has important consequences for our problem of the expression of our responsibility to our neighbor. For this means that the first and primary thing that is required of me, if I am to act in love, is not that I try to impose myself or my ideas on the other as though I were God with absolute truth in my hand, but that I accept the other as a person, as one who has his own integrity in his own right. Above all else I must not violate or lead him to violate his own convictions and the integrity of his own personal existence, which he (as I myself) has from and before God. We cannot excuse ourselves from this second aspect of love through saying that it is only the person of the fellow Christian whom we must treat with such respect, that the person of the sinner who is outside the fold is to be preached to with no such concerns. For this is to violate the nature of love as it is revealed to us in the New Testament. God does not honor the freedom and integrity only of believers, acting as a dictatorial tyrant toward sinners. God does not force sinners to turn toward him against their will. It is just the sinner whom God loves so much that he actually sacrifices himself so that the sinner, in his own freedom and out of the gratitude welling up within him, may turn to God. If God's *agape* is the model of the love expected of the Christian, then we must always act toward even the worst sinner with the utmost respect for him as a personal being, one who is himself responsible to God.

This means that in our attempt to love our neighbor, there must not be, in the first place, condemnation of the other for his ideas or his actions or his very being, but rather acceptance of the other as a fellow creature of God for whom Christ also died, acceptance of him as a brother. Our brotherly concern for him will not lead us to begin immediately with condemning him for his sins; rather, it will lead us to try sympathetically to understand his situation as he himself understands it, and thus to try to appreciate his own efforts to see the truth and the right and to live by them, however much these efforts may differ from or even contradict our own position. As Christians we will not insist on his living in the precise relation to God which happens to be our own, for this would be trying to play the role of the Mediator ourselves, trying to be the Christ. We will rather be concerned that his own unique and independent relation to God through Christ be deepened. As Christians, our love will not express itself through the attempt to make our brother over in our own image—this is the epitome of sin. It will express itself rather in our acceptance of him as he is, whoever he is—and even our making ourselves as much like him as we can—in the hope that thus may we be the instrument through which God may transform him into *his will*—something possibly quite different from *our conception* of his will for our brother. "For though I am free from all men, I have made myself a slave to all, that I might win the more. To the Jews I became as a Jew, in order to win Jews; to those under the law I became as one under the law—though not being myself under the law—that I might win those under the law. To those outside the law I became as one outside the law—not being without law toward God but under the law of Christ—that I might win those outside the law. To the weak I became weak, that I might win the weak. I have become all things to all men, that I might by all means save some" (1 Cor. 9:19-22).

The second aspect, then—though first in order of importance—of our love for our neighbor is the acceptance of him as a person, giving full honor to his insights into the truth and the right and his duty, trying to help him deepen his own relationship with God in Christ, rather than simply making him into our own disciple. For those of us who are heir to the Anabaptist-Mennonite tradition, with its insistence on the theological necessity for religious liberty, this should be a self-evident point. It has, nevertheless, some hard consequences for us. In regard to the problem of nonresistance specifically, it implies that we have no right—if we are truly disciples of Christ acting out of love—to preach from the housetops that *we* have the true faith and the true understanding of the Christian life, all others to the contrary notwithstanding. It means just the opposite. It means that we must express our love to our neighbor, whether he claims to be Christian or not, through first listening to his understanding of what is demanded of him by God. It means that we must be more concerned to help him to see clearly the implications of his own insights into God's commands than to denounce him for not interpreting God's commands as we interpret them. It means our first concern must be for his integrity as a responsible agent before God, not for our interpretation of the gospel. For freedom and spontaneity and openness in his relationship to God, Christ has set him free; let us be careful, therefore, that we do not attempt to impose upon him a new yoke of slavery to our ideas of what that relationship to God should entail (Gal. 5:1).

Most Christian pacifists, I suppose, would accept in substance what has been said here, at least as it applies to cases of individual counseling in which they become involved. Thus if a young man, troubled about whether he should go into the army or become a conscientious objector, asks help, most pacifists would do all they could to help him come to a clearer and deeper understanding of what his own convictions already are and what the implications of those convictions might be for his present decision. Beyond this, most pacifists would no doubt try to explain their own understanding of the implications of the Christian faith on the issue of war, and would try to help him see why they think a pacifist position is required of a Christian. *But surely no one has the right to say to the other: this is what you must decide; this is God's will for you.* The decision as to what he must do is something which each must make for himself in his own confrontation with the God who made himself known in Jesus Christ. No one else has the right to play the role of the Mediator and to tell him what God requires of him. Nor does anyone else have the right to relieve him of the responsibility of making his own decision himself and bearing the consequences thereof. To do so is to attempt to dominate the other—the very reversal of love—and to try to frustrate his attempt to be the responsible and free person which God has created him to be. To do so is to demand that a man decide and live by a faith which is not his own, and the consequences of which, therefore, he will not be prepared to bear, ending, as they have in the past and may again in the future, in the cross. To do so is to forget that "Christian discipleship is a matter of individual calling and response," and therefore we should "not expect Christian ethics of the non-Christian."[5]

This has important implications, also, for our attitude toward society, and our expectations of society. Societies, as well as individuals, are guided in their actions by moral insights and appreciation of moral values; and hence, in a certain sense, societies also must be treated as free and responsible moral agents. Thus, the sensitivity to moral values in American society is such that enslavement of other humans is no longer acceptable to that society as a whole (though it might well be to many individuals in the society), and this sensitivity has become incorporated in the laws and customs and mores of the society. On the other hand, the sensitivity of our society to economic inequalities and injustices and to the horrors of atomic warfare is not as highly developed as in some other contemporary nations. The actions of our nation, as of all nations, result not only from the power factors that play around it, but also from the context of moral values and insights carried and kept alive in the mores, customs, and laws of the country, a context which provides norms in terms of which the nation "decides" what it "ought to do" in the circumstances confronting it. This context is of course never precisely definable, nor is it the same in all parts of the community. The mores of the deep South are somewhat different from the North on the matter of relations between the races, and the mores of one small homogeneous community, e.g., the Hutterites, may be quite at variance from those of the surrounding peoples. But despite all variations and ambiguities, the context is always there as a factor whenever a community or society acts as a social unit. Societies, as well as individuals, may be sensitive to and responsive to moral insights and values and even to the demands of God laid upon them. Because of this capacity, societies also may be sinful. Not only the Christian church but every social group must be understood as such a morally and religiously responsible agent.[6]

As Christians, therefore, our attitude toward the actions and beliefs of a society, whether our own or some other, must be analogous to our attitude toward a fellow man who has come to us for counsel. Before preaching fiery denunciations of the evil and sin which we see before us, we must lovingly and sympathetically attempt to *accept* what is before us in all its sinfulness. We must attempt to *understand* what are the insights and the values which govern the society and try to see what it means to live believing them to come from God himself. We must, in other words, be just as sympathetic and understanding, and just as unwilling to impose our own will, on the society of which we are a part, as we would be in the case of an individual whom we truly love. Our desire here, as there, must be to help the society come to a deeper understanding of *its own* deepest convictions before God, and help it to see more clearly the implications of the various courses of action which lie before it. For example, we must not, as too often pacifists have, simply witness against every military bill that comes before Congress. This is indeed part of our obligation, our obligation to witness. But we who know well that it is folly to expect non-Christians to act as Christians, and to expect Christians whose understanding of the faith is of one sort to act as Christians whose understanding of the faith is different, ought to know that it is folly to expect our nation to demilitarize completely. We ought, therefore, to be prepared, along with our negative witness, to *support* the military bill most in accord with the highest ideals and best moral insights of the total American society. Americans as a whole do not believe in defenselessness or nonresistance, and to demand that they act as if they did is not only folly, it is positively immoral; for this is to demand that others in our nation live by our faith, our understanding of the will of God, rather than their own. *If we would truly be disciples who would love, we must go beyond merely witnessing to our faith. We must concern ourselves with attempting to help our nation come to a deeper understanding of her own faith, her own convictions, the moral insights which are the context in terms of which she lives and acts. And we must attempt to help her come to a decision and work out a course of action in terms of her faith, rather than our own, however*

*much we might desire her to follow what we believe to be the right.*
This of course does not mean that our obligation to witness to God's
requirement of nonresistant love is in any wise eliminated or even
diminished; rather, this points toward the context which we must
continuously maintain if that witnessing is truly to be witnessing in
love. Any other course than this in the case of the nation of which we
are a part—just as in the case of an individual friend—is motivated
not so much by real self-giving love as by the desire to dominate and
impose our will, the precise opposite of love.

Christian love of the neighbor, then, whether that neighbor be
considered as an individual or whether he be viewed collectively as a
society, must always have at least these two aspects if it is to be love at
all. It must involve a sincere and honest and forthright witness for the
truth and the right as God enables us to see the truth and the right.
But it must also involve a sincere acceptance of the other as God has
given him to us in all his frailties and weaknesses and sin, with the
determined effort to help him apprehend more clearly the insights
into the truth and the right which God has given him and the effort to
help him make the decision in his own free and responsible relation
before God.

### III.

There is also a third aspect of the way in which love expresses itself,
and this is in many ways the most difficult and paradoxical of all. If
we truly love the other, we cannot forsake him even when he decides
in a way which we take to be wrong and sinful; we must continue to
love him as a person and attempt to help him live up to his own
insights even when those insights contradict ours. That is to say, we
must support him as a person who in the integrity of his own
convictions and the depth of his own conscience has come to a
decision and is now following out a course of action which we think to
be wrong. Again God's love must be our model. God does not forsake
man even when he decides against him and pursues a course of action
which is sinful and disobedient. In his faithfulness God continues to
love the sinner and seeks to redeem him. The whole Old Testament is
the story of God's faithfulness with Israel through all manner of
betrayals. Finally, when Israel seems to be a hopeless case, instead of
letting her go, God in his love goes beyond anything he has done
before and sacrifices of himself. Agape is just that which is never
stopped by rebuffs, which never gives up. The more impossible the
situation, the more effort love expends to redeem the offender. From
this point of view the practice of the ban and excommunication
(except out of love for the offender) is certainly highly questionable,
and the question of church discipline, however necessary it may
appear to be, becomes a very difficult issue indeed. We who are

imperfect and sinful judges of our neighbor should think long indeed before we cast him out from the community and cease to love and serve him. In such action is our love really the love of God? Is our faithfulness really an expression of his?

We cannot, then, forsake the one who has decided in a manner which we think to be wrong. We must in fact seek to uphold him in his own convictions, even while we are trying to help him come to deeper insight into the implications of the gospel. As Paul points out in the controversy over eating meats offered to idols, even when one is convinced the other is wrong, he has no right to make him violate his conscience, which would be to cause him to sin. "Thus, sinning against your brethren and wounding their conscience when it is weak, you sin against Christ" (1 Cor. 8:12; cf. 10:28). This of course does not mean that we are to support all others in everything that they do, for humans, ourselves included, do much out of simple selfishness and sin or plain unconcern, and for this are to be condemned. But it does mean that when we are convinced that the other is acting in accordance with the deepest insights of his conscience, we must support and encourage him in that action. In such a case we certainly have no right to break off fellowship with him. When my friend, then, concludes that it is his Christian duty to join the army, I have no right, on the basis of my own understanding of the Christian gospel in any way to hinder him from obeying the scruples of his conscience, and thus by my "knowledge" actually to destroy this Christian brother (1 Cor. 8:11). Nor is it enough merely to refrain from hindering him. As one who loves his brother, I must do all I can to help and support him in his resolution, to make it possible for him to live according to the insights of his conscience as God has given him those insights. As Christians, after all, our concern is first and foremost with love rather than knowledge. This means that our concern must be for the self-integrity of the person of our fellow before God, in the first place, and only secondly for our own knowledge or understanding of what the gospel is or implies. We should always beware lest this secondary concern be infected with our own pride in understanding so that in our emphasis on it we have lost the real personal concern of love for our fellow.

This third aspect of love, which goes out to and stays with the one who appears to us to be acting sinfully even in his act of sin, also has important implications for our action as members of a society. The deepest convictions of our society *which is not a Christian society* (in the Mennonite sense of the word) are not fully Christian in character, though they have been influenced by Christian ideals and values. Therefore, we should not expect the course of action which our society follows to be identical with the kind of action which a society of Christians of the Mennonite persuasion might follow. This, however, gives us no leave to withdraw from society and to refuse to participate in its decisions or to support it in the actions to which it is finally led. Nor does this give us leave simply to "witness" to our faith. Rather, if we are truly acting out of love, we must enter into the situation, helping our society come to the best decision of which it is capable in the light of the value insights and ideals carried in the mores, and then support it as best we can in carrying out this decision. Anything less than this would be dogmatic insistence that our society should act according to our knowledge rather than its own, and should exemplify the convictions of our conscience rather than its own. Or, to put it another way, it would involve our expecting our nation to go against its own best knowledge, and if you please, to violate its own conscience. Wounding even the weak conscience of our brethren is a sin against Christ, as Paul reminds us (1 Cor. 8:12). As Christians, then, we have no right to withdraw from even the most horribly unchristian (as it seems to us) decisions which our nation finds itself facing, and we have no right to withdraw from support of the course of action to which it is led, if that action is in accord with the nation's best insights. Instead, we must constantly be attempting to help our nation come to the very best decision of which it is capable (and this will no doubt not be a pacifist decision in the case of war), through not only witnessing to our own understanding of the demands God lays upon us and the nation, but also through helping our nation become more clearly aware of its own highest convictions. This will involve our participating in the actual formulation of policy, for without such participation, our help is only abstract and unreal. The policy which we must help to formulate will not be the kind of policy we might formulate were we acting as members of a Mennonite society; it will be a policy in line with the ideals of the nation in which we are working. To refuse to do this is to refuse to help our nation to live up to the best that it now knows: it is to refuse to love our neighbor and to assist him in living in moral integrity.

Having aided in the formulation of policy, we must not shy away from also helping to implement it. For this would be to refuse to help our nation stand by its convictions; it would be backing out at just the moment when the greatest support is necessary. This does not mean supporting our nation merely in courses of action with which we happen to agree. It means supporting it in the best courses of action of which it is itself morally capable, and these will include many things with which we disagree, such as, no doubt, a large defense budget. The kind of participation and support which is here envisaged may well require running for Congress and voting "yes" on bills which personally violate one's own convictions; it may require holding office in the State Department (or even the Defense Department), if in such capacity one can really aid one's nation in acting as morally as it is possible for it to act. It does not allow withdrawal from any level of political responsibility simply to keep one's own hands clean, if it is clear that through acting in that position we might help our fellow Americans somehow more nearly to serve Christ's cause—more nearly to act in accordance with the demands which God places upon them—than would otherwise be the case. Our concern must at all points be a concern for helping the nation to come closer to doing what it ought to do, and if this would seem to require great sacrifice on our own part—even the sacrifice of dirtying our hands a little or a great deal—love is always prepared to make whatever sacrifice is required for the sake of the brethren, especially those brethren who are not yet Christian. Our concern for our people as a nation and a society should be so great that we ought to be willing to say with Paul: "For I could wish that I myself were accursed and cut off from Christ for the sake of my brethren, my kinsmen by race" (Rom. 9:3, RSV). Our love for our fellows should be so great that we should be willing to give up all—even Christ—if this would help to bring them closer to him in understanding and action.

Upon first consideration, it may seem that what is being advocated here is a form of compromise, but this is emphatically not the case. There is no place for compromise in the Christian ethic, if compromise be interpreted as some kind of voluntary sacrifice of the requirements of love to enable action in some other fashion. Love is just that which has adequate resources within itself—the very resources of God himself—to make it possible to meet with and deal with every situation which it confronts in all its variety and all its sinfulness. Without compromising itself at any point, love is able to adapt itself to the needs of every situation it encounters. Love thus never becomes a rigid absolute, the ethical implications of which are clearly and absolutely defined for every situation. This is to turn love into its opposite and to live by law instead of love. Love is just that which has sufficient power in itself to live in openness and freedom and flexibility adapting its response to every situation and to the needs which the situation itself presents[7] without ever losing its own true character as love. It is only a weak defensiveness, unsure of itself and certainly unloving, which is unwilling to face every situation as it comes, and to deal with its needs in terms of those needs themselves, rather than in terms of some pat formula which arbitrarily defines what the needs must be and what the answer to them must be. "The absoluteness of love is its power to go into the concrete situation, to discover what is demanded by the predicament of the concrete to which it turns."[8]

## IV.

In attempting to deal with the situation in its own terms, love, then, is not compromising itself, but simply being its own true nature—radical, self-giving concern for the neighbor. Such radical concern, as we have seen, must always in every action have the neighbor's welfare at heart; it must always be devoted to helping the neighbor achieve morally and religiously the most of which he is capable. This concern, as we have seen, must express itself in at least three aspects simultaneously. Firstly, it is essential that we always try to communicate to the neighbor the best and deepest understanding of the Christian gospel and its implications of which we are capable, i.e., we must "witness" as vigorously, forthrightly, and honestly as we can to our understanding of God's gift and God's demand. This witness must be both in private life and conversation, and through public proclamation and action in the society as a whole. We must do all we can to deepen the insights and elevate the ideals of our neighbor and of the society of which we are a part. Secondly, we must do our utmost to help our neighbor and our nation come to an understanding of the way God is already confronting them in the ideals and values and convictions which are already to some extent honored. We must thus try to help the neighbor see more clearly what his own convictions are and what the implications of those convictions are for the present situation of decision with which he is faced. These convictions will no doubt not be Christian in the sense in which we understand the word, but they are nevertheless the way in which God is now making his demands known to the neighbor through his own conscience. Thirdly, we must encourage and support our neighbor and our nation and help them to follow the course of action most nearly consonant with their best ideals. As members of a democratic society who have the possibility and the responsibility of participating in government, we must do all we can to help the nation act as morally as the present level of its convictions will permit. On the personal level this calls for support of the other in his conscientious decision; on the national level, this calls for participation in the social and political processes whenever and wherever through such participation we might help our nation to act more responsibly to God.

It is of course evident that in any given concrete situation there may well be conflicts among these three aspects of the demands of love upon us. Thus, on a complicated issue like national conscription, a pacifist Christian may have to take what, seen from without, appear to be contradictory positions, but which in reality are an expression of the way in which love seeks the highest possible level of moral activity in every situation. It would certainly be necessary for the pacifist to witness to his convictions about the wrongness and evilness of war. Such witness might express itself in letter writing, in speeches, in refusing to register for the draft, or in a variety of other ways. It must be made clear that the Christian does not rely on force of arms in this world, but on God, even though this leads to a cross, as it did in its most noteworthy exemplification. At the same time, it must be made clear that this nonresistance is not based on any pragmatic conviction that it will win the war or melt the hearts of the enemy or anything else of that sort. It is based on the eschatological conviction at the very heart of Christian faith that the future is in the hands of the God who made himself known in Jesus Christ, and that therefore we can accept whatever that future might bring without regard for ourselves, even though it bring a cross.

But the pacifist Christian cannot stop with this witness. He is well aware of the fact that his nation as a whole and most of the individuals in it do not live by this eschatological faith. They do, however, share certain ideals about justice being better than injustice, about tyranny and slavery being worse than freedom. Though it is of course to be hoped that some might heed the witness of the pacifist Christian, he knows that not many will, and he therefore does not expect the nation as a whole to adopt a policy of defenselessness in the international world, as much as he might desire this. This gives him no justification for withdrawal from the situation, having made his witness. Rather, it means that he must, alongside of his other witness, also help his countrymen to come to an understanding of their own convictions about justice and tyranny as relevant to the problem of conscription. Certainly a militaristic system in which the burdens are shared as equally as possible among the people is preferable to one which puts the burdens on the helpless or the poor. The pacifist Christian might therefore support through letters, speeches, votes, and so forth, certain military programs as more just and less tyrannical than alternative ones, and certain tax programs for supporting the military as more desirable than others. Were it even possible to secure it, a truly sensitive Christian would not advocate that his nation adopt as policy some such "pacifist" program as unilateral disarmament, for he would know full well that this was not in accord with the convictions of the people; and when the test would come, they would not have the eschatological faith necessary for them to face the cross, but might fall subject to anarchy or tyranny.

The Christian, then, in the second place, must attempt to help the people see and adopt the program most nearly consonant with their convictions. This could conceivably lead to the paradox of a Christian writing to his congressmen to vote in favor of a given conscription bill as the most adequate for the nation as a whole, but himself finding it necessary to refuse to register under that same bill in order to bear his witness to his deepest Christian convictions. And though he himself be jailed for his noncooperation with the government's program, he might nevertheless find it necessary to support his country's efforts, e.g., to limit the expansion of Russia, as the best expression of the nation's own convictions at present attainable. Despite the external appearance of contradiction, there is no reason why a pacifist Christian could not hold even the highest offices of his nation during wartime, for his obligation out of love is to act responsibly in the situation in which he finds God has actually placed him. In this case this means he must help his people act as morally as they can under the circumstances of war, and he might be more effective in such high office than anywhere else. And yet, at the same time, he would somehow have to make known his conviction that judged by the higher standard of the Christian revelation, which is neither known nor accepted by the nation as a whole, the nation's program is under God's judgment. The Christian does not compromise with love when he is doing his utmost to help his society to act as morally as it can; he compromises with love when he is unwilling to take the risk of being in the world, though not of it, through attempting to withdraw from participation in the social order. Such withdrawal is the worst possible compromise, because it attempts to fulfill the first aspect of love, witnessing, while neglecting the others. Love must find a way to fulfill all three of these aspects in every situation if it is to be the love which is revealed in the New Testament. That this will be exceedingly difficult in nearly every situation, and that different persons and different communities will come to different conclusions about just how this threefold demand is to be met in any given situation, is evident. But this should not surprise Christians, for we know well that even though our knowledge of the situation in which we live and of the gospel itself, as well as our expectations and prophecies about what is to come, is imperfect and must ultimately pass away, nevertheless love will never cease or be destroyed (1 Cor. 13:8-13).

## V.

A word may be added about certain further theological implications and presuppositions of the position here taken. Yoder has argued for the recognition of a dualistic principle in Christian ethics which takes seriously the dichotomy between church and world, Christian and non-Christian action.[9] The present essay has tried to take seriously the existence of this dichotomy, but without drawing the conclusion that this implies that the church need not "assume responsibility for the moral structure of non-Christian society."[10] Rather, as God's agent here on earth—the very body of Christ—the church has absolute responsibility for the moral structure and activity of all of the world. There is indeed a dichotomy between church and world, between those who consciously seek to serve Christ, and those who only unconsciously are subject to his lordship.[11] But this dichotomy is not an objective dichotomy the boundaries of which are clearly apparent to Christians; it is not a dichotomy of condemnation through which the church identifies and condemns the world from which it then may separate itself. The parable of the tares (Matt. 13:24-30) should remind us that no human eyes are sharp enough to make such distinctions; the separation of the wheat from the tares must await the Last Judgment. This dichotomy is a subjective dichotomy in the consciousness of the Christian. It is a dichotomy of understanding by means of which the Christian and the church are enabled to distinguish and appreciate the difference between the world and themselves and thus be prepared out of love to act in accordance with such distinctions. Instead of providing the basis for a judgment on the world which is forbidden us (Matt. 7:1-5), it provides the basis for *understanding* the world, its actions, and thus dealing with it in love.

This difference in understanding of the meaning of the dichotomy has important theological implications for both the doctrine of man and the doctrine of God. Whereas the *dichotomy of condemnation* can easily betray us into the sin of pride in thinking that we are Christian and hence better than others who are of the world, and thus tends toward *breaking down* personal relations rather than building them in the manner of love, the *dichotomy of understanding* leads us to see that though there is indeed a true distinction between tares and wheat, they are so intermixed in this world that we must confess that both are in us, i.e., that sin and the world are also present in those of in the church. (This is certainly the position of the whole New Testament.) Thus the dichotomy of understanding leads to and is an expression of humility, while the dichotomy of condemnation leads to and is an expression of spiritual pride. We must come to see that the power structures opposing love, which we as Christians must oppose in the name of love, are not only to be found in the world but also in the church, and particularly in the operation of such practices as the ban and excommunication, where all the social power the community can muster is often directed *against* the offender, rather than in love for him. Furthermore, we must come to understand that we often unwittingly participate in the power structures of the world with no protest. Thus, as Mennonites, though we have voiced protest against war, we have readily participated in the use of economic power against our employers or employees or competitors with practically no protest at all. Our witness to love has been too exclusively political and military; we have taken the other aspects of social life for granted, and the world is therefore in us. The dichotomy of understanding helps us to see that in many ways we are so much a part of each other that the kind of withdrawal presupposed by and advocated by the dichotomy of condemnation is not only immoral, but impossible. It does not take due account of the radical solidarity of man, a solidarity presupposed by both the doctrines of the Fall in Adam and redemption through Christ.

The dichotomy of condemnation leads not only to a false division in human nature, but to a destruction of the very unity of God. For God is seen as acting in radically different, and even contradictory, ways in relation to humankind: ". . . in the order of conservation, He uses the violent state to punish evil with evil to preserve a degree of order in society and leave room for His higher working in the order of redemption, through nonresistant self-giving love in Christians."[12] Since God's being and action are inseparable, this kind of dichotomizing makes God into a being of hate and violence as well as love and redemption, a dualism certainly with no basis in the New Testament, where God reveals himself as *agape*; and a dualism which the doctrine of the Trinity was formulated specifically to overcome. Instead of thus dividing the divine being, it is theologically much more adequate to interpret the different ways in which God deals with humankind as his *loving* adaptation of his will to the great variations in humanity's moral needs, moral insights, and moral capabilities, so that even when God uses the violence of the state—or a revolution against the state for that matter—in his dealings with humankind, he is doing so out of his love for them. (Cf. Luther's notion of the "strange work" of God's love.) This is certainly the way in which violent and warlike actions attributed to God in the Old Testament are to be understood, and the same holds for God's dealings with humanity since the time of Christ in situations where the revelation of Christ is not known or appropriated, and where humanity's situation is thus analogous to that under the Old Covenant. Thus the different modes of God's relations to and with the church and the world should be understood in terms of God's will to work redemptively in and with both the church and the world. The differences are due to God's understanding of man's differences, i.e. the differences here also ought to be interpreted in terms of the dichotomy of understanding guiding the expression of the divine redemptive love, rather than as an implication of a dichotomy of condemnation in which is expressed an opposition between a God of violence and a God of love. If it be said that this view does not take account of God's judgment, that is not true. Judgment is certainly involved, for example, in the way those who take the sword perish by the sword, but it is always essential to understand even such judgment as an expression of the divine redemptive love, which is God's essence.

[1] Niebuhr's position is set forth in various places. See especially *An Interpretation of Christian Ethics* (New York: Harper and Bros., 1935), and "Why the Christian Church Is Not Pacifist," in *Christianity and Power Politics* (New York: Scribners, 1940). His most recent statement on the subject appears in an article written in collaboration with Angus Dun in *Christianity and Crisis*, June 13, 1955, "God Wills Both Justice and Peace."

[2] See especially John Howard Yoder's articles, "Reinhold Niebuhr and Christian Pacifism," in *Mennonite Quarterly Review* (1955) 29:101-117, and "The Anabaptist Dissent: The Logic of the Place of the Disciple in Society," in *Concern*, a pamphlet series, no. 1 (1954), pp. 45-68.

[3] It should be evident from this discussion that the notion of "responsibility" as a category of Christian ethics is neither simply an axiom which is taken for granted but has no theological basis, nor does it find its theological justification in terms of a doctrine of sin. Yoder seems to think these are the roots of the notion of responsibility (cf. "The Anabaptist Dissent," *op. cit.,* especially pp. 57 ff.) though elsewhere ("Reinhold Niebuhr and Christian Pacifism," *op. cit.,* p. 113), while also arguing this view, he admits that "there exists a real Christian responsibility for the social order, but that responsibility is a derivative of Christian love...." This is essentially the position I am maintaining, and some implications of which I am trying to develop.

[4] *The Divine Imperative,* (Philadelphia: Westminster Press, 1947), p. 129.

[5] Yoder, "The Anabaptist Dissent," *op. cit.,* p. 46.

[6] This treatment of every society as a moral agent and as morally responsible is certainly biblically justified. Not only is Israel treated thus but also the surrounding nations. (See especially Amos 1-2 as well as the other prophets.) In the biblical view of man there is no such radical separation of individual from group as we modern individualists like to maintain. (See especially, J. Pedersen, *Israel, Its Life and Culture* I-II [London: G. Cumberlege, Oxford University Press, 1926-40], H. W. Robinson, *Inspiration and Revelation in the Old Testament* [Oxford: Clarendon Press, 1946], pp. 70 ff., etc.) The interpretation of society as a morally responsible agent is also ethically required, inasmuch as the persons we are to love are never really separable from the society of which they are a part (as rationalistic individualists would like to believe), and we cannot, therefore, love the *whole person* and minister to him without concerning ourselves with the social involvements which are a part of him. A society is after all a new moral unit brought about by the social relationships of persons with each other.

[7] From this point of view, Yoder's contention that "right action can be identical for all" ("Reinhold Niebuhr and Christian Pacifism," *op. cit.,* p. 114.) is not only so abstract as to be meaningless in understanding the problems of moral decision and action, it is directly counter to the nature of love which always takes account of the concrete needs of the other toward which the action is directed and the situation or context of the action. Since the needs and the situation are different in crucial respects for every decision and action, this statement becomes either a summary of the rigid ethics of law or else a purely formal statement to the effect that right action is always loving action.

[8] Paul Tillich, *Systematic Theology I* (Chicago: University of Chicago Press, 1951), p. 152.

[9] "The Anabaptist Dissent," *op. cit.,* esp. pp. 50 ff.

[10] *Ibid.,* p. 46.

[11] *Ibid.,* pp. 54 ff.

[12] *Ibid.,* p. 51.

# Chapter 6

# Christian Decision Making*

Christian faith understands itself as rooted in the loving action of the God who has created the world and who has brought into being in the course of history a community which knows his love and seeks to respond to it, thus becoming its vehicle in human affairs. God's ultimate purpose for history is the creation of his kingdom—the community of perfect love within which individuals can become truly free and creative, fulfilling God's original purposes for man.

The church knows—as a kind of foretaste of the kingdom—something of the quality of love and the possibilities of real freedom and creativity for which she believes humankind is destined. Her hope and expectation that God will make these anticipations the very substance of human existence make possible such loving self-sacrifice, and freedom from legal codes and other idolatries, as she knows in her present existence. It is in this hope that the church lives in those moments when she actually becomes the community destined finally to be the kingdom of God. And it is in this hope that individuals within the church live in those moments when they become genuinely free spirits, able to give themselves in love to friends and enemies alike. In this sense the Christian hope, itself rooted in the Christian faith, is the essential ground and basis for all Christian deciding and acting: the Christian ethic is an eschatological ethic.

We must attempt now to see what these observations mean for the practical day-to-day decisions with which the Christian individual

*From *The Context of Decision* (New York: Abingdon Press, 1961), pp. 89-93, 97-120.

and community are faced. However, it must be emphasized that in considering so-called practical problems we will not be resolving the moral dilemma. The Christian life is above all a free life, one in which each takes upon himself the responsibility before God for his own decisions. There can, therefore, be no final answers to any genuine moral problems; indeed, there cannot even be settled questions. Only for perspectives other than faith in the living God can issues be settled in advance. For a faith that understands it must ever be responsive to God's love in accordance with the unique character of each historical situation, it is never possible to lay down rules. One can only live in continuous receptiveness to the will of God and in living responsiveness to every need of the neighbor, and then freely and creatively decide in each moment to do what appears required of love for that moment, always taking reponsibility for one's action. With this forewarning, that we will be unable to settle any "practical" questions in advance because such questions can be settled, as the word suggests, only in *practice,* that is, in *actual decision and action,* we proceed to an analysis of the problem of deciding and acting.

## I.

The Christian of course (whether individual or community) does not come to this matter of practical action *de novo.* Every decision occurs within the context of an ongoing historical process. One comes to every new decision having made previous decisions which have shaped one's character in certain ways and have obligated one to others in various ways. One always comes as a person with previous commitments—to family, to friends, to nation, to church, to many other communities, to God. And it is in terms of these commitments that the present decision must inevitably be made. This means that every decision will be complex and difficult, for failure to honor one's prior obligations is to break faith with other persons, to disrupt community with them. Though this may be necessary on occasion, it is difficult to justify from the point of view of an ethic whose primary concern is the building of real community among people. Moreover, the diversity of commitments in which different individuals and communities are involved will necessarily mean that what is "right" for one individual or group may not be right for some other. It may well be right for a surgeon in certain circumstances to open a man's chest and operate on his heart; it is doubtful if it would ever be right for me to do so. The situation in which one stands, one's own aptitudes and prior commitments, the freedom of the Christian before God, and the adaptability of love itself to every possible situation, all mean that Christian decisions can never be governed by inflexible rules.

But from this it does not follow that no principles or guides for decision making can be suggested. Indeed, such a position would reduce the Christian ethic to practical acceptance of the *status quo,* when in fact it involves radical rejection of every *status quo* in favor of the demands of the kingdom of God. How, then, do the demands of the kingdom impinge upon us in concrete terms? What concrete demands are laid upon me in my every moment of decision? The general answer to these questions, of course, is that I am required to give myself in love without reservation to neighbor and enemy alike. But our question is: What now, in my actual moments of choice, does love require me to do?

This is not something to be answered simply on the basis of our vague intuitions or definite conceptions of love; it is to be answered, so far as possible, in terms of God's revelation to us of what love is and requires. "In this is love," writes the author of the first letter of John, "not that we loved God but that he loved us and sent his Son to be the expiation for our sins" (4:10, RSV). The model of love in terms of which we must reach our decisions is God's act of self-giving in Jesus Christ. If we take seriously the notion that God has here revealed himself and his will, it will be this alone which we will seek to make determinative of our decisions. Although in our continuous failure to obey his will other factors drawn from our sinful selves and situations will also become effectual, our conscious effort must ever be directed toward deciding and acting solely in terms of the obligations laid on us in God's revelation. To take any position other than this would be to deny either that God has actually revealed his will for us, or that it is in fact God—the creator of our being and Lord of our destiny—whose will has been made known.

## II.

Christian love always seeks to act both creatively and redemptively with and for persons imprisoned in sin and suffering, and this it does with eyes exclusively on the need of the other, with no concern for the needs of the self. This is what is required of every Christian individual and community whenever called to make a decision—which is to say, in every moment.

But this still does not tell us what we ought to do in the concrete choices each of us faces every moment. Were there only two people in the world, myself and another, it would go a long way toward giving such guidance. For in that situation the principal moral question would be: How can I serve the other's true interests most effectively? Even these decisions would not always be easy, for in our finite ignorance we seldom know precisely what kind of response the other needs from us. Few parents, for example, know when and precisely how they ought to punish their child so as not to injure or embitter his personality but help him grow into a creative and loving person.

But, however simple or difficult these questions might be in a world of two persons, it is obvious they become almost infinitely complicated merely by introducing a third. Such a change means far more than a mere doubling of the problems. Now a whole new order of problems is introduced: How am I to divide my time and efforts between these two confronting me? Each has different needs and different capacities; how do I allow for this? To take an extreme example, were one an idiot and the other a genius, I obviously would have to act in very different ways toward each, giving one what I denied the other. But by what principle could these decisions be made? Doubtless my efforts to build community among ourselves would meet with diverse responses from these differing individuals. But what could be done about this? Should I give greater time and attention to the one who is more responsive, or to the other? It seems I ought to respond to the former's love with a fuller giving of myself to him; but on the other hand, it is apparently the unresponsive one who actually needs my love the more.

In some situations I might have to choose between my two friends. To take an extreme case again—but one critical for the problem of Christian nonresistance—I might one day come upon the one in the act of shooting the other. What should I do now? If I myself shoot Cain, who has gun in hand, I destroy all possibilities of further giving myself in love to him; if I do not, he will shoot Abel, and then I no longer can serve him. Since Cain is evidently more in need of redemptive love, perhaps I should refrain from shooting; but certainly this seems both unjust and unloving to Abel who has been responsive to my love with love of his own. What, then, does love require me to do?

It should be clear from this example that merely to say we should love absolutely does not resolve the problem of decision, even in a world consisting of only three persons. In the actual world of several billion, the problems of decision are multiplied beyond imagination. We are responsible, somehow, to meet human need anywhere and everywhere we find it; we are obligated to love everyone. How is it possible to make choices in this kind of situation? Clearly, to respond to God's will responsibly we need some principles of selection, enabling us to give preference to certain claims while rejecting others. For without such selection we could not act at all. It is on this issue that the widest disagreements among Christian moralists in the contemporary scene are to be found. Few responsible writers would question the absoluteness of the obligation to love laid on the Christian. Few would question that this obligation directs us into situations of sin and suffering. The disputed and unresolved issue concerns this matter of actual preference and selection in the concrete choices which we must make.

It is commonly held[1] that this problem can and should be resolved by reference to the standard of justice. Whereas love is appropriate and meaningful in personal face-to-face relations, justice, precisely because it is more abstract and general, is impartial and objective, and thus appropriate to large-scale social relations. Situations that require me to decide between the needs of several neighbors, therefore, should be dealt with in terms of justice. Although love, conceived as absolute self-giving, may be significant and relevant in close personal relations, when applied to the problems of the social order, it is at best an "impossible possibility."[2]

There is no time here to give this position the full analysis it deserves. I can only point out that introducing the category of justice does not, as is supposed, in any way lessen the problem of preferential decisions in a complex social order. For the problem simply reappears in the form of the question: How can I be just to everyone everywhere? How is it possible for me to deal impartially with every person when I do not and cannot have relations with more than a few? The principle of justice taken by itself is of no more help in the concrete problems of decision making than is the command to love. If it has seemed so, that is because its less radical character—allowing a place for the needs and desires of the self, along with the needs of the neighbor—makes justice appear a more feasible objective. But we have really only transposed the problem of concrete decision making, not resolved it, to say nothing of the fact that in watering down love to the level of justice, we have tempered God's wisdom with our foolishness. We must, then, return to Christian love and ask if any principles of preference arise immanently out of it.

### III.

It appears to me that four considerations, deriving from the Christian revelation of God's love for us in our sin, can be isolated and significantly discussed in this context. Though neither separately nor collectively will they present us with *the* answer to any concrete problem of moral decision, each calls our attention to certain critical questions that should be considered in every decision. As will be seen, these considerations exist in a certain tension with each other, and this tension is never resolved except in the moment of decision itself.

One of these matters, justice, has already been mentioned. Though considerations of justice do not resolve the problem of decision making, they must enter into every decision for the sake of love itself. For love demands that I give myself to the needs of every person, not simply this one or that one. There is no one whom I have the right to exclude from my love. Not that I am required to deal with each in the same way; that would be unloving. The needs of people are different, and love must minister in accordance with need. But all people I confront have needs to which I can minister, and my ministrations cannot be governed by partiality and favoritism, but must be the expression of justice. This can be seen clearly in the family. The parents ought to love all the children in some sense equally. It would be unjust, and thus unloving, for them to play favorites, showering attention on one and ignoring another. The demand for justice here is a demand of love itself. But precisely because it is demanded by *love,* it is clear this can be no even-handed justice which gives precisely the same *thing* to every child. Rather, as love, it will seek to meet the unique and individual needs of each child.

From this demand for justice arising from love itself, there derives a quasi-utilitarian principle which, when explicitly formulated, can be a guide in making decisions. One ought to do whatever will serve to the highest degree the genuine needs of the greatest number of persons. On the surface, this principle may appear to be a concise expression of the implications for social ethics of the Christian imperative to love, and it has often been so interpreted. However, as we shall see, though one authentic strand of those implications is laid bare here, the matter is really far more complex than this simple formula suggests.

The requirement of justice in our loving is not the only one we must consider. A second consideration, of at least equal importance, has to do with the special responsibilities belonging to every individual and every group. There are several sorts of special responsibilities that are relevant here. In the first place, I have responsibilities deriving from my particular aptitudes and talents. "Every one to whom much is given, of him will much be required" (Luke 12:48). If I have special musical aptitudes, I should not seek to serve my neighbor through digging ditches; if I am awkward with my hands, I should not seek to become a surgeon. One's peculiar talents and aptitudes open up special opportunities not accessible to others. In a community of love each should serve in accordance with his unique gifts. As Paul put it: "Now there are varieties of gifts, but the same Spirit; and there are varieties of service, but the same Lord; and there are varieties of working, but it is the same God who inspires them all in every one. To each is given the manifestation of the Spirit for the common good" (1 Cor. 12:4-7, RSV).

A second kind of special responsibilities devolves from the promises and commitments we have made. Promising is the act of binding the self to another for some future time. When I have promised to meet another at a particular time and place, I have laid on myself a special obligation to see that the meeting is kept. Moreover, this obligation takes a certain precedence over other responsibilities that might arise as I am on the road to the meeting place. Not that the obligation is absolute, so that I must "pass by on the other side" if I meet a man who has been beaten almost to death. But certainly love obliges me to keep the appointment if possible, lest I break faith with the other. Our lives are filled with special obligations rooted this way in commitments made to others and to ourselves. Some such obligations are trivial, but some are momentous, as with the promise to live one's entire life with another.

Closely related to the special responsibilities that are mine by virtue of my peculiar aptitudes or particular promises, are those that fall to me because of the roles I play in society. When I get married I take up a new role, the role of husband. In so doing I obligate myself not only to my wife to whom I promise responsible performance of the duties of this role, but also to society at large which defines for me and my wife what it is to be a husband in twentieth-century America—something quite different from, e.g., contemporary China, or ancient Israel. Of course one plays many roles simultaneously and with each go special responsibilities. As a father I have particular obligations to my own children which I do not have to others: I am charged in a special way with their care and upbringing. As a son I have particular obligations to my parents which I do not have with respect to other adults. As a teacher I have a special responsibility for my students which I do not have for everyone I meet on the street. If I were a doctor, I would have particular responsibilities to the sick; if a newspaper editor, to my readers; if a merchant, to those who bought from me. We always play definite roles in the various communities in which we participate, and these roles lay upon us special responsibilities which we are obligated to discharge.

The important point to note here is that these responsibilities must often be given priority in our decisions over the claims of the first consideration we mentioned, justice. It is clear that we do not and we ought not to treat our own children precisely the same way we treat everyone else's. It is my particular obligation to care for my children and to aid their development into mature selves. Though certainly I cannot neglect the demands of justice and ignore the needs of other children, I am required to give a certain preference to my own: if I do not, I am simply refusing to be a father to them. If I try to be a father to everyone, I will only succeed in being a father to no one. Each of us must seek to play the special roles to which we as individuals have been called. This is the only way we can actually love anyone at all, for as finite creatures we cannot serve more than a few effectively.

This understanding—that each of us can in fact serve in love only relatively few persons to whom we are related in our special responsibilities—underlies the Protestant doctrine of vocation. Each is called by God to his particular tasks in society, and there he must work if he would serve the neighbor. No one else can be the father to my children: this is my task. No one else can teach my students that which I have been called to teach them. This is my vocation in God's kingdom, shaped partly by my aptitudes and training, partly by promises I have made, partly by my role as defined by society. If I do not fill my role, no one will. God's will that I love and serve my neighbors can be obeyed in this *present moment* only through loving these neighbors whom I confront *here and now in this situation,* and whom I can serve through the particular roles I am here called upon to play. Trying to love everyone equally—as one might suppose abstract justice requires—results in loving no one at all.

It should be clear, then, that the commandment to love involves consideration both of justice and the full range of our various special responsibilities. All demand consideration; none can be ignored. Often, perhaps always, they exist in tension with each other, and we have to forsake some demands to fulfill others. But we can never reduce them to each other, for they are incommensurable. In every situation the demands of each should be weighed against the others before a decision is made. Furthermore, in each new situation there must be a new weighing and a new decision.

These considerations by themselves, then, never tell us the *right* action. It is the act of decision that finally determines what course of action shall be followed in freedom. Thus, we alone are responsible for what we decide, and we cannot avoid bearing that responsibility. However, these considerations do call our attention to requirements of love we might otherwise overlook.

The matters of justice and special responsibilities, however, have not yet brought us to the heart of the Christian conception of love. For the distinctive thing about Christian love is its overriding concern for the sinful. In the parable of the prodigal son, instead of carefully ascertaining that justice be done to both sons—the one punished and the other rewarded—love forgives the sinner and forgets the requirements of justice entirely (Luke 15:11-32). And, to drive home the point, Jesus states explicitly that "there will be more joy in heaven over one sinner who repents than over ninety-nine righteous persons who need no repentance" (Luke 15:7, RSV). Obviously, this great concern for the sinful and evil which is at the very heart of redemptive love must seriously qualify what we have said thus far. It is conceivable that in certain situations justice and special responsibilities may have to be disregarded in the name of love for the sinner. For example, though these two considerations seem to require one to defend his family against a murderer, it may be that a Christian ought to have greater concern for the redemption of the murderer than for the safety of his family. Certainly forgetting to love the murderer is not justifiable, simply because of fear for one's family. "If you love those who love you, what credit is that to you? For even sinners love those who love them. . . . But love your enemies, and do good . . . expecting nothing in return . . . and you will be sons of the Most High" (Luke 6:32, 35, RSV). There is a strong imperative in love toward precisely the one whom we would be inclined to overlook if we took account only of the requirements of justice and our responsibilities. This third consideration we can designate, for the sake of brevity, the concern for redemption.

The introduction of this matter does not mean, however, that the others can be ignored. They also flow from love, and it is no more justifiable to overlook their demands than to forget love for the sinner. In every situation we must weigh each of these three factors against the others in reaching our decision. It is clear they will often be in tension, pulling us in diverse ways. We are forced inevitably at such times deliberately to ignore or compromise certain of the *apparent* obligations laid upon us by love, in the attempt to do what we have concluded love *really* requires of us. Obviously, in this kind of complex situation of conflicting obligations there will be no clear-cut right choice. Nevertheless, we alone must take the responsibility for our choice, for it will be no one's decision but ours.

There is a fourth consideration that must be brought into the situation of decision. This is the matter of the distinctively Christian self-knowledge that we are sinners. If this is indeed self-knowledge— and not merely a dogma nominally subscribed to—we will know that all of our decisions proceed from our sinful involvement in selfish interests, and that we must, therefore, take special care lest we convince ourselves we are acting from love when in fact we are not. Christians will be aware of their tendencies to delude themselves with rationalizations and will guard against such. We will know, for example, that in a conflict between our responsibilities to our families and the requirements of justice or concern for the sinner, we often convince ourselves to forget the latter two. Thus a parent selfishly favors his own children, gives them privileges and opportunities, instead of working, for example, for integrated schools and equal opportunities for all children. Again, in a war situation if justice seems to require that we support our nation, we may forget our obligation to love the enemy.

There is not time to multiply examples. The point should be clear. Whenever we are faced with a decision, we will be sorely tempted to take the easier, more self-centered way, and to rationalize away the more difficult claims of love. And this fact, also, must be taken into account in difficult decisions: we must lean over backwards in the direction we would prefer to avoid, in order to allow for our sinful perverseness.

There are, then, at least these four incommensurable matters which must be considered whenever a serious decision is made—all of them required by the imperative that we give ourselves absolutely out of love for our fellows. None can be ignored; none can be reduced to the others. Nor can they be reduced to numerical values and then added up together in the manner of some utilitarian calculus, getting a sum which tells us the "right" thing to do. Every decision requires a kind of intuitive estimate of the claims of each consideration and then a deliberate preferring of one or more to the others. It is the immeasurability and incommensurability of these matters that make every crucial decision what we always know it to be in the hour we are faced with the choice: a kind of stab in the dark or leap into the unknown in which we hope and pray we do the right, but which we always well know may be the wrong.

## IV.

We now have before us in abstract terms the problem which the Christian faces in reaching decisions genuinely responsive to the will of God. In order to make clearer the relevance of this analysis to the actual making of decisions, it is necessary to consider briefly a concrete problem. Almost any significant current issue would be appropriate here—race relations, academic freedom, our agricultural surplus in a hungry world, and so on. However, as the historic peace churches have always understood, the issues for the Christian conscience are perhaps most sharply pointed up by the problem of Christian participation in war. Let us see what light our analysis throws on some of the dimensions of this complex issue.

It should be clear from our discussion thus far that no legalistic solution to this problem can be given for two reasons: First, no legalistic answer prescribing in advance the "right" course of action can be given to any problem faced by the Christian. Such would deny the freedom of both God and man and make the relation between them—in this case at least—one of law. And this would violate the very heart of the gospel. Second, the issues in such a complicated question as participation in the defense of one's nation are obviously complex and ambiguous, involving very real tensions between the various considerations we have isolated. Such tensions will be resolved in differing ways by different Christians, the several considerations impressing themselves upon them variously. It is, therefore, not possible to legislate a final "right" answer to the problems involved here. Each Christian must personally bear responsibility before God for his resolution of the issues.

Remembering these qualifications, however, we can briefly try to see what is involved in the question. What light do our four considerations throw on the problem of Christian participation in war?

The implication of the matter of justice, taken simply by itself, is relatively clear. It requires one to align oneself with the side, the victory of which, so far as he can tell, will bring more good, or less evil, to more people. Often, of course, it is difficult to make such judgments, but when possible, the demand of justice is obvious.

But complications in this position arise as soon as we remember our third consideration, redemption. Redemptive love is concerned for the sinner. But how does one redeem a sinner through bombing him? How does one reconcile people—so alienated from God and from their fellows as to become aggressors in war—through destroying them? It might still be possible to work redemptively with survivors at the end of a war, but what about those killed? Even if there were an answer to this question, what right has one to kill some in order to redeem others? Though justice—as well as one's special responsibilities to those aggressed against—might seem to require one to fight the aggressor, it is not clear how this can be reconciled with love's demand to work redemptively with sinners. Justice apparently requires us to take sides; redemption seems to question the very possibility of violently opposing aggression.

Further complications enter the picture when one remembers the fourth consideration. If my own nation is at war, clearly my self-interest is involved in her success or failure. In this kind of situation it becomes extraordinarily easy to convince oneself that our side is the just side; we are in the right. The fact that both sides rationalize thus—hardly anyone fighting against his own nation in the conviction that the enemy has the just cause—should qualify one's estimate of the claims of justice in the matter. Is it not likely that the claims of self-interest are the really effective ones here?

Clearly, none of these matters can be assessed certainly and irrevocably. Therefore, it should not surprise us that faithful and honest Christians have disagreed on the proper role for Christians in wartime. Some have concluded it to be their duty to participate in the war effort; others, that they must refuse.

It is necessary at this point to turn to our second consideration, the matter of special responsibilities. In some cases these may conclusively affect the decision. Consider, for example, a Christian who holds the position of secretary of state. When he takes up such a position he takes upon himself the special responsibility to care for the needs of the nation, seeking to preserve it against destruction, and the like. He has responsibilities here by virtue both of the role he is in and the promises he made when taking office. Obviously, as a Christian, he must also be concerned about justice for all people and the redemption of sinners. But when he is working in and through his office, love would seem to require that he give his official commitments priority over these other considerations: to do otherwise would be to break faith with those for whom he has promised to decide and act. And in taking up his office he has agreed to perform precisely this task of making decisions for the nation as a whole.

Clearly the special responsibilities of the secretary of state will require that he seek to avoid war, but it is not clear that he has the right to do so at all costs, e.g., at the cost of slavery, if such is not in accord with the will of the majority of those for whom he must decide. His responsibilities, then, will probably require him to advocate a substantial defense budget, to make defensive alliances against potential aggressors, and the like. The wholesale destructiveness of nuclear warfare certainly complicates these issues enormously, but this problem cannot be discussed here. The important point to note is that most of his *official* decisions will have to be made in the light of his special responsibilities in any case *precisely because those decisions are derivative from and an expression of those responsibilities.* (This in turn implies, of course, that decisions stemming more directly from other roles must in a similar way be appropriate to *them*—here "pacifist" convictions, e.g., might become controlling. However impossible it may be to separate absolutely the various roles played by any one person, they must be clearly distinguished in order to grasp the real moral issues involved in each.) The secretary of state is the man who has been placed by the nation in a position to make decisions for the nation as a whole. If the nation were largely pacifist, it would be irresponsible for him to develop a large defense program. But in a nonpacifist nation—as in twentieth-century America—it would be a failure to fulfill the demands of Christian love upon him, were he to work out a "pacifist" foreign policy. Thus, many of the decisions of a Christian secretary of state will be guided simply by his best judgment on how the responsibilities of his office are to be carried out—though he must make some place also for the claims of justice and redemption.

In contrast, now, with the man in a responsible government post, consider the ordinary Christian citizen. Only a very few of his activities, such as voting and paying taxes, involve special responsibilities to the nation as a whole. None of his activities involve such responsibilities in the way the acts of a government official do. *For he is never in the position of being required to make decisions in behalf of the whole nation.* Thus, in his decisions special responsibilities to the nation cannot weigh so heavily as with the government officer. Accordingly, the considerations of justice and redemption will enter with more weight into his deliberations. Perhaps he will find that he must refuse to enter the army when drafted, that, on the contrary, he must publicize the evils of war, seeking to sensitize American consciences in regard to its unchristian character, that he must engage in relief and rehabilitation work, and the like. In short, he may become a conscientious objector.

Because of an awareness of the responsibilities of public office, sectarian groups such as the Mennonites have often concluded that a serious Christian cannot participate in government. It is not difficult to see why they have drawn this conclusion. Since a public official must be responsible to all the people—not only to serious Christians—he is unable in his *official* actions to witness very clearly to the radical character of the Christian ethic. Both sectarian thinkers and those who hold that Christians must take responsibility for society have interpreted this fact as the "compromise" which is inevitable when one seeks to apply Christian love to the social order. On the basis of this judgment the former group have called for withdrawal of Christians from responsible positions in society; the latter have regarded "compromise" as a necessary evil.

Both positions are in error. For both have misconstrued as "compromise" the fact that love, in seeking to serve the *other,* must always *relate itself to that other in his actual situation,* whatever be its character. Both, in short, have understood love primarily as *law* (a fixed form of action) rather than as *freedom* (creatively adapting itself to meet the real needs of every situation). When Christian love is understood in terms of Christian freedom, then it becomes clear that the "right" course of action cannot be laid down in any law but must be reached in responsible decision before God. This requires that we take account of love's demand for justice *and* redemption *and* the fulfilling of our special responsibilities. To argue otherwise is to forsake the Christian gospel and the freedom for which Christ has set us free (Gal. 5:1), and to substitute for them a new legalism and thus a new slavery. As Paul rightly says of such legalistic Christians: "You are severed from Christ, you who would be justified by the law; you have fallen away from grace" (5:4, RSV).

Far from being compromise, it is precisely the radical demand of the Christian ethic, to love without self-concern, that may require one to serve his fellows through government position. As Paul reminds us, "there is no [governmental] authority except from God, and those that exist have been instituted by God" (Rom. 13:1). It is by means of government that God orders people in their social relationships. Moreover, in our own time of welfare services, public schools, and the like, there is no question that great and good services are performed through governmental channels, and in certain cases (e.g., in time of economic depression), can only be performed in this way. And this being the case, undoubtedly the special aptitudes, interests, and training of some persons make it their Christian duty before God to enter political life. Moreover, there is no reason in principle why they should not accept such responsible and difficult positions as secretary of state or the presidency. Indeed, *if it is in this role that one can most effectively serve one's fellowmen, it is precisely to this role that one is called by Christian love,* however ambiguous and difficult and contrary to one's private convictions may be the decisions required from time to time. God's command is that we love our neighbor regardless of the kind of situation into which this brings us, not that we squeamishly protect our own moral scruples in order not to dirty our hands. If we really love, we must, as Paul put it, even prepare to be "accursed and cut off from Christ for the sake of [our] brethren" (Rom. 9:3), our fellow citizens. We must be willing to decide and act in whatever situation God leads us.

Whatever one's views about Christian pacifism in general may be, it is clear that the complex issues here cannot be settled *either pro or con* simply in the abstract. To do so is to neglect what is of central importance for Christian love: the moral demands of the concrete situation in which I am called to decide and act. Right action here as elsewhere cannot be determined by some abstract principle—whether of loyal service in defense of one's nation, or of conscientious objection to all involvement in such activity—but only in conscientious decision in the situation itself. Such decision will always seek not mere consistency with principles, but rather to be responsible to the will of God for that moment, responsive to the radical demands of Christian love in that situation. However, this much at least is clear: no serious Christian may make a decision involving the issues raised by Christian pacifism without giving the most careful consideration to the radical and perhaps undesired responsibilities here laid on the Christian.

It is clear that—although nonresistant love is always the appropriate response of the Christian individual and group to God's love (and for this reason straightforward nonpacifism as well as "vocational pacifism" must be regarded as inadequate interpretations of the Christian ethic)—because of love's concern for redemption, withdrawal from the evils of society cannot be justified. In the light of Christian freedom, Christian love can be seen as living and plastic in such a way that it both remains nonresistant and yet can take up real reponsibilities in the social order.

## V.

We can conclude this brief sketch of the ambiguities and difficulties of the problem of decision by recalling once again the context which gives decision meaning. However careful the deliberation which precedes it, decision as we have noted in this chapter always involves a leap into the unknown. We may develop guides and principles to help us discern the ramifications of the alternatives confronting us, but the choice itself—the act through which we eliminate certain alternatives with their proper claims and select the one to which we will give ourselves—is entirely our own doing, and we alone must bear responsibility for it. If the only context for our decisions were the confusing welter of claims and counterclaims of our various special responsibilities, of justice, and of redemption, the constant imperative to decide might well lead to despair. But for Christian faith no such result need follow—indeed the contrary is the case. For within the threefold context of Christian life, acts of decision have genuine meaning as the real fulfillment of authentic human existence. This context may be summarily sketched as follows:

First, the ultimate reality with which men have to do—God—is a genuinely meaningful foundation for establishing the significance of human decisions and actions; for he is apprehended in faith as himself free and creative, loving and forgiving. He has called this world into existence that there might be a community of love and freedom, and he is working out this purpose in the actual course of history.

Second, Christian faith is aware of the concrete actualization of this purpose in a community of genuine love and forgiveness—the church. This community, with its tradition reporting "the mighty acts of God" and its expectation of the coming kingdom of God, provides a haven of purpose and meaning within the otherwise chaotic course of human history.

Third, the Christian knows himself to be called into existence as a free and creative being, redeemed from bondage to the failures and sin of the past in order to realize his freedom within the beloved community. Therefore the leap of decision in freedom and love through which he creatively takes upon himself responsibility for his action is just the moment of his fulfillment, his redemption, his genuine rapport with the purposes of God. It is precisely in the full realization of his freedom that man, as an active and responsible creator, finally becomes what God intended him to be—the image of the Creator himself (Gen. 1:27).

Thus, whereas the imperative to decision might well lead to despair were its only context the social and cultural chaos of relative claims and values, within the context provided by Christian faith, it is just this opportunity to decide, to create, and to bear responsibility for action, that is apprehended as authentic human existence.

## VI.

It might be thought that this analysis of the freedom and relativity of Christian decision making implies there is no proper place for such groups as the Mennonites, who insist that Christian love must always express itself in radical nonresistance. But this is not so. The Anabaptist founders of the Mennonite tradition well knew that

Christian freedom was the presupposition of the position they took. This is why they insisted that church and state must be separate and the church be a "believers' church." The church can be the church only when people freely and openly and consciously decide to respond to God's act of love in Jesus Christ through loving their fellow human beings. But the implication of this view that both the foundation and the fruition of the Christian community are found in God's calling people in and to freedom is diversity and variety within the Christian church. For in their freedom people inevitably understand and respond to God's call in diverse ways. To expect anything else would be to suppose God had created a community of puppets, all cut from the same mold and all acting in the same ways. We should not be surprised, then, to find within the Christian church at large what in fact we do find: a group of subcommunities each clinging to some significant aspect of the gospel which God has enabled them, in their freedom, to see and confess.

The Mennonite church is one such subcommunity. We in this tradition stand here because in our faith we have freely decided this is the position to which God's command has led us, namely, to die martyrs' deaths—if God grant us the strength—before we bear arms against a fellow human being. We dare not abandon these convictions; we dare not give up our witness. To do so would be to disobey God's will as we have come to know that will for us. But by the same token, we dare not deny other Christians the right, indeed the duty, to remind us of other facets of the gospel which we may have overlooked and which may contradict our interpretation of God's will. We dare not fail to recognize as Christian brother he who conscientiously and honestly and freely before God concludes that Christian love requires him to participate in the defense of his nation. It may be that because of our differences, we cannot witness to the gospel within the same subcommunity in the Christian church. It may be that for the Mennonite community to make its peculiar and essential witness to the rest of the church and the world, it will find necessary the exercise of a discipline which excludes from its immediate fellowship persons of alien conviction. But, as we saw in an earlier chapter, if such action seems required, we should not regard it as more than a pragmatic act, necessary to make a clear witness on this issue which seems to Mennonites central to the Christian faith. No claims beyond that can be made. Indeed, it is essential that every group which knows itself to be the bearer of a unique and perhaps indispensable interpretation of the Christian gospel forthrightly accept in Christian love and fellowship those other subcommunities within the church with which it differs.

God and God's kingdom are more and greater than any of us in our subcommunities within the Christian church can know or imagine.

He, after all, is the creator of the heavens and the earth, and we are simply his very limited and sinful creatures. God's revelation is so rich and so full that no human interpretations—or combination of human interpretations—can hold it. It overflows all. Hence, the diversity of views among Christians on theological and moral issues, together with its concrete sociological expression in the variety of subcommunities within the Christian church, is something for which we should be grateful. It is God's way of giving himself to us, not simply in the partiality and incompleteness of our own convictions, however strong and essential they may seem to us to be, but in the wholeness of the faith of the whole church.

There is no call, then, for all denominational groups to forsake the convictions to which they have historically witnessed simply because they have come to realize it is also possible for Christians to witness to contrary convictions. On the contrary, they must forthrightly and openly witness to those convictions which God has granted them— both to church and to world. For only as they make such a witness to the others whom God is also calling, is there justification for their separate existence as distinct communions.

This is not the place to attempt an assessment of the peculiar tasks to which each of the various significant subtraditions within Christendom has been called. If we truly believe in God's providence, it will be clear to us that he has been preserving each for some significant purpose within his church. For the Mennonite community, I would venture to say, that purpose for our day is to become a living witness—in and to the rest of the church—to the demand of love to forsake all defenses of every sort, acting in every sinful and evil situation with real healing and redemption. Were Mennonites to carry out this witness—not in the pride of being the only true Christians but in the humility of being, before God, fellow sinners with the rest—perhaps God would enable them to speak with real effect, and other Christians from other subcommunities within the church would, in their freedom, come also to see this as the will of God for them.

[1]See, e.g., Reinhold Niebuhr *Moral Man and Immoral Society* (New York: Scribners, 1932) and *Interpretation of Christian Ethics* (New York: Harper, 1935); E. Brunner, *Divine Imperative* (Philadelphia: Westminster Press, 1947) and *Justice and the Social Order* (New York: Harper, 1945); P. Ramsey, *Basic Christian Ethics* (New York: Scribners, 1950).

[2]See, e.g., Niebuhr, *Interpretation of Christian Ethics,* Ch. 4.

# Part Three:

# CHRISTIAN PARTICIPATION IN SECULAR SOCIETY

# Chapter 7

# The Christian in Church and World*

Several years ago I published an article in *Concern* on "Nonresistance and Responsibility" (ch. 5 of the present volume). This was accompanied by a critical discussion by Albert Meyer,[1] and followed, in the next issue, by further criticism from David Habegger.[2] It was expected that the conversation would be continued, but I did not submit a rejoinder to the two critical articles. The discussion of the problems continued, however, for subsequently I published two books[3] dealing directly or indirectly with some of the issues raised in the several articles, and now recently there has appeared a long and careful review of *The Context of Decision* by John Howard Yoder,[4] raising anew certain problems with my position. I do not intend to take up each of the many questions that have been raised in these several places. That would not further the discussion in any systematic or orderly way and would be tedious and pedantic as well. What seems appropriate at this time is for me to attempt to deal afresh with the central issues that have arisen in these various discussions.

All of the issues appear to me to be aspects of one crucial problem, the relation of the church and/or the individual Christian to the world in which they find themselves. Though perhaps not all would go so far as to say that the church's very existence is for the world—in the sense that the church is here as the continuing wedge of God's act to save the world—all parties would agree, I think, that a major portion of the church's business here on earth is with the world.

---

*This article, written in 1963, was not previously published.

Christians are called upon to witness to God's saving act in Christ, to love and serve others as God has loved them. The church, therefore, cannot sit in some sort of splendid isolation and purity and remain Christ's church. She must enter into the world of rebellion against God with her ministry of reconciliation in the consciousness that precisely this historical activity of hers is the very vehicle of God's reconciling act (2 Cor. 5:20). All participants to the discussion, then, appear to be agreed that whatever justification there may have been for historic Mennonite tendencies to withdraw from society at large, such practices are not appropriate for our time. The crucial differences would seem to arise at several points within this basic agreement: (1) There are differences in understanding of the character and possibilities of the church, within this church-world relationship. (2) The actual sociological involvement of the individual Christian in the church and in other societies is apparently understood in quite different ways. (3) In consequence, the way in which the individual Christian and the empirical church as well are *in* the world—i.e., bound up with the world—and must take a certain responsibility for that world is conceived and formulated quite differently. On each of these points, I believe, my critics have tried to hold to a more traditional Mennonite position, which their commitment to active involvement with the world actually belies. I have simply tried to carry through, in what seems to me a consistent fashion, the implications of an ethic of radical nonresistant discipleship when one sees this necessarily leads us *into* the world rather than away from it. The fact that this has led me somewhat farther from certain traditional Mennonite formulations than some of my critics, will not, I hope, lead anyone to think that we are not all engaged in a common task: that of thinking through afresh the meaning and significance of our Mennonite understanding of the Christian faith for the terrifying world in which we in the middle of the twentieth century live.

(1) *The church in the world.* Mennonites have liked to think of themselves as *in* but not *of* the world. This formulation has, however, come to hide more of the truth from us than it has revealed. For it has suggested that the church's ground and basis were other than and independent of the historical context in which the church found herself. Even as a sociological and historical entity, the church, it has seemed, can and does live simply and directly from God. Though she is surrounded by other institutions and communities, they in no way nourish or sustain her. On the contrary, they are the evil world which she must combat with all her might, even while she is seeking to evangelize and convert such souls as will hear her witness.

In addition to being sociologically ridiculous, this conception has serious theological weaknesses. It fails, for example, to reckon with the radically historical character of God's acts and of Christian faith. For, instead of seeing how the present living church has its life from past stages of the church's history—going back not only through the Reformation, but on through medieval Catholicism, the period of the ecumenical councils and of Constantine, to the primitive church and finally to the person-event Jesus Christ—this view suggests the sustaining life in the church arises out of some immediate and direct relation to God. But in fact for Christian faith every redemptive relation to God is mediated historically, i.e., through God's historical act in the historical Jesus Christ, an act carried down to us through the living movement of church history. If these historical connections which bind us to the rest of the church and church history are once perceived, then it becomes clear that whatever living "in but not of" the world means, it cannot mean living as congregations unsustained by empirical historical ties to the rest of Christendom. On the contrary, the very life of every congregation is given from the greater church history from which it springs.

Not only is the church dependent on its own past, on Christian history, it is also radically dependent on the society in which it lives, a fact we have been even less willing to recognize. It is clear that, with the exception of certain rare cases, the church has not understood itself as called to fulfill all of the functions of society. Thus, many political and social functions, such as planning, building and maintenance of roads and other forms of transportation, developing mail services and other networks of communication, the general ordering of society and keeping of the peace, have been left to other institutions in the social order. But the church continually uses these and in fact depends upon them for its very existence. The church has almost always depended upon the existing economic institutions of society to make it possible for its members to sustain themselves physically (Paul was a tentmaker!) as well as for the church as an institution to provide itself with such material needs (e.g., buildings, books, educational materials, etc.) as it had. (Even the Hutterian Brethren buy and sell commodities in the outside economic markets, and thus depend heavily on the economic order round about them.) Nor does the New Testament church ever conceive itself as separated from the world in any absolute sense. Paul who (to quote some favorite Mennonite passages) told the Corinthians not to "be mismated with unbelievers" but to "come out from them, and be separate from them" (2 Cor. 6:14, 17, RSV), also made it very clear that this did not mean the church was somehow to withdraw from society completely "since then you would need to go out of the world" (1 Cor. 5:10, RSV)—a notion which apparently seems simply absurd to Paul. The church, thus, is connected by many and various bonds to society-at-large, and these, in fact, in part sustain it in being. If we are to deal at all realistically with the problem of the relation of church and world, it is necessary that we understand the full implications of this historico-sociological—and theological!—fact.

While Catholicism appears to have understood these dimensions of the historicalness of Christianity best, and sectarian Christianity least, sectarian traditions have seen most clearly the other side of our historicity: that precisely the church's historicalness means that every member thereof is called to the radical historical decision to put all his energies in the service of those currents through which God is creating his kingdom in and through history. And so we have demanded believer's baptism, radical discipleship, a church committed to its Lord and not to the ebb and flow of the tides of secular history and society. All of this is to the good. The church can be nothing significant if it is not a committed church of committed individuals. From this point of view it is clear there must be effective church discipline of some sort, not only for the sake of the church but also for the members who are always prone to slip back into easier and less strenuous ethical postures if they are not continually reminded and encouraged by their brethren to strive for the highest. (Such discipline, it goes without saying, should always be conducted in a loving spirit and for the sake of the offender; it is hardly justifiable simply to separate him from the community because of the feared contamination of his presence. In practicing such discipline, it must be admitted, there are great dangers of self-righteousness and self-delusion, sins which have often characterized Mennonite discipline in the past.) The church, then, precisely because it is the point in history and society through which God's redemptive act is breaking into history and overcoming the historical forces which oppose it, must be a committed and disciplined community, as the Anabaptists clearly understood (though most of the "church-type" churches have failed to grasp and insist on this).

Now the problem of what the church is and how it can be what it is, lies in a proper grasping of these two sides of its historicity: its radical dependence on its past and on the society in which it is found, and the radical demand laid upon it to decide for and help to create a new and different future for itself and for the world. There is not space here to work out in detail the implications of this two-sided historicalness of the church. Suffice it to emphasize one point: any interpretation which portrays church and world simply as radically opposed to each other is a vast oversimplification (one which perhaps even the biblical writers engaged in upon occasion for polemical purposes). Church and world are quite as much mutually *de*pendent as they are *in*dependent. The world needs the church for its salvation from utter destruction, for the church is the historical current within the world which is moving it toward the "beloved community" which is God's kingdom. In this sense the church is "the soul of the world" (Diognetus). But the church needs the world to give it real, substantial—yes, material and empirical—existence, lest it be a soul with no body, which is nothing. For the church is really nothing but transformed world, world in the process of being transformed into God's kingdom, and thus a part of the world become the historical instrument of that very transformation (see chapter 4 above).

If the church is thus not a separate society from the world, but rather that aspect of the world through which God is transforming human history into his kingdom, then the critical question becomes not, How can or should the church separate itself from the evil or non-Christian tendencies or elements in society? but rather, How and when does the church in fact become the instrument of God's redemptive transformative work? To this question there is, I think (for Mennonites at least), a clear and definitive answer, however complicated and ambiguous may be the attempt to give it practical expression: In the cross, God has revealed to us both the method through which he works redemptively, and the price he exacts of us. It is in and through self-sacrificing love, which bears the evil others have inflicted upon it, that God works to overcome the evil in this world, transforming it into his kingdom. And we are called to be instruments of precisely that same redemptive love regardless of the cost to ourselves. Even though such wholehearted self-giving may seem naive or foolish—or may appear to forget what seem to us to be the demands of justice or righteousness—we who are Christians have no choice but to follow this path. *For to say that in the cross God revealed his nature and will is to say that here and here alone is to be found the revelation of true justice and righteousness; this image of absolute self-giving is the ultimate norm for all decision and action.* (For this reason I cannot accept David Habegger's [quasi-Calvinist] view that there is some sort of righteousness beyond or independent of or even separate from the self-giving love we see on the cross.[5] Such a position implies and presupposes a revelation more final and authoritative than Jesus Christ.) The unique theological importance of the Anabaptist-Mennonite tradition arises out of its understanding from the beginning the radical implications of subjecting all human insights and standards to the norm revealed in the cross. Radical discipleship means precisely that we let this critical point in human history, which overturns even many Old Testament ideas and beliefs, become our norm and standard, however much some other view might appear more prudent or reasonable or desirable.

The church, then, is that society which seeks to live by and exemplify and promote precisely this redemptive nonresistant love that overturns all human conceptions and values. For the church is that society which is convinced that it is in just such an overturning that God is transforming this rebellious order into his obedient kingdom. Thus the church cannot oppose the world in the sense of fight the world, for to do so would be to use the very methods of the world—power and violence—which God is seeking to overcome through his nonresistance; nor can she ignore the world. Rather, her very life is found precisely in her laying down her life *for* the world in the hope that thus will God succeed in redeeming the world. It is in this way and this respect *alone* that the church is *in* but not *of* the world.

(2) *The individual Christian in the church and in other societies.* The interconnection between church and world is, however, much more complicated than I have yet succeeded in stating. For thus far the discussion has proceeded as if there were two entities, *church,* and *world,* which could be defined over against and in relation to each other. Certainly some of the language of the New Testament appears to suggest that the church thus is a kind of "body," a unified organism with definite boundaries demarking it and setting it off clearly from its environment. But the metaphors must not be taken too literally here, lest they conceal from us the very reality toward which they point. It is clear that the church, if it is an organism at all, is of a special sort: it is a *social* organism, not a *physical* one. That is, it is a community of persons, not a physical body. And though for certain purposes it may be useful to liken a community to a physical organism, in order, for example, to show the functional interdependence and even the indispensability of each of the various members (as Paul does in 1 Cor.), it would be a bad error to suppose that such a metaphor adequately defined all of the essential aspects of the Christian community. Living and free persons in a community of love have a certain autonomy and independence which the organs of a body never achieve. The organs exist and can exist only in and for the body: they enjoy no sort of independent or private life of their own; and especially, it must be emphasized, they have no *inner* life of their own. Free persons, however, who live in community together, do so at least in part out of the free and independent decision of each individual to bind himself to the others in service and love, and out of the steadfast purpose of each individual to stay in this way bound. (This understanding of the church's necessary rootage in the decisions and steadfast wills of its members was, of course, a central contention of the Anabaptists.)

But this means that there is a certain "looseness" in the organic structure of the church as compared with a physical organism. If the church were the *total* society in which the individual is immersed (which, as we have seen above, is far from the case), then this looseness would be minimized, for all of the vital relationships in which an individual lives would be within the body of the church, and the individual's total life would thus be churchly. As it is, however, many of a person's vital relations (economic, political, social) are extra-ecclesiastical. One lives in and is sustained by a variety of communities and owes much to each. One's life and responsibilities, then, cannot rightly be defined simply by reference to the church. Each of these other communities must be taken into account as well. Thus it is highly misleading to say, as Albert Meyer does, that "the Christian . . . is willing to make an open commitment and to take sides, *even if that means a certain unavoidable separation from all societies* but that unique society, the church of Christ."[6] It was precisely this sort of totalitarian view of the church in relation to all other human groups that led to such extreme rigorism among some early Anabaptists that even marriage and home could be destroyed at command of the elders or the congregation. If the actual church were ideal—i.e., were in fact the kingdom of God in its fullness and glory present here on earth—then the totality of one's existence could and should properly be lived therein. But in the human history which we have known and know, this is never the case; and it is simply self-delusion, if not highly immoral, to pretend this ideality and to act on that pretension. No society within history is an entity so separated from all other societies that it is possible or right to commit oneself to it alone, and this is least of all true of the church, the very body on earth of the One through whom God is acting "to reconcile to himself *all* things, whether on earth or in heaven" (Col. 1:20, RSV). Although it is certainly necessary to emphasize the distinction and difference of church and world, and the differences in our obligations to each, the matter is far more complicated and subtle than some easy highsounding statements imply. Were the church a physical instead of a social organism, and were the church not here for the express purpose of serving the world, different conclusions might be drawn.

I cannot go much further here in sketching out these complex sociological interrelations. We must, however, consider certain of the implications of the fact that in part this complexity arises out of the fact that the individuals who are members of the church are also members of other societies; moreover, it is precisely through these multiple memberships that the church is able to have a living impact on the world (as well as vice versa). Thus the businessman who is a Christian is able to bring a significant witness into the economic world (though all too often this has been a witness more to a certain type of piety than to the import of the Christian faith for the whole economic order); the teacher who is a Christian is in a position to be the living contact between the church and the educational institution; etc. Without the great variety of such contacts and connections, bringing the church into relationship with every social stratum and social group, the church would not be *in* the world at all—and thus would not even be. And certainly there would be no way in which she could perform her mission to be the instrument through which God is transforming the world.

But all of this means, of course, that the members of the church who live in these multiple relationships must share in the responsibilities of the various societies to which they belong. A teacher who refuses to take upon himself the obligations and responsibilities and commitments and values of the teaching profession will not be able to function effectively in that profession for long; a physician who refuses to accept the norms and standards of the medical profession as the proper way to order his medical activity will soon be regarded as a charlatan. The various societies to which we belong each have their ordering principles and values and we are able to work within those societies as able and respected (and thus potentially influential) members only if we abide by the rules. This, of course, does not mean that we cannot act to change the rules: all societies have accepted means for amending their practices and their principles. But we have to act here, also, largely in accordance with the procedures acceptable to the society itself, or we simply find ourselves cast out with no voice at all—salt no longer capable of salting.

Now all of this is, I think, more or less self-evident, but we Mennonites have not taken it very seriously in thinking out our ethic of the individual Christian as a member of the church and of other societies. Instead we have adopted in theory a kind of ecclesiastical imperialism, though of course in practice we have often allowed the norms of other social groups to exercise full sway over our members—e.g., in business, or medicine, or farming, or education, or even, in some cases, in politics or the military, though here we have been most suspicious. I think it is high time we thought out our theory anew on this question, not to bring it into accord with our practice— heaven preserve us from that!—but to make it realistic and significant in the sociological situation in which we find ourselves. It is necessary for us to think through carefully: (a) the way in which church and world are actually interrelated through members of the church being at the same time members of other societies (this is a sociological problem); (b) the obligations and responsibilities one owes to these extra-ecclesiastical societies to which one belongs (this is both a sociological and an ethical problem and one which we Mennonites have almost completely neglected); so that (c) we can understand and define more precisely and meaningfully the way in which the individual Christian is to order his life and make his decisions vis-a-vis the church and the other societies in which he lives; and (d) we will be able to come to a fuller and more significant understanding of the actual relation between church and world, and thus can become a more effective church in the world.

In this brief paper I can make only a few comments on these matters, focusing primarily on (c). If what I have said above about the actual involvement of the Christian in extra-ecclesiastical societies is correct, then it follows that the kind of ecclesiastical imperialism which demands that the individual disciple make his decisions exclusively in terms of the concrete norms of the empirical living church is unacceptable. The existing church can no longer be regarded as *the* norm-giving society, *the* society to which and in terms of which one's life is oriented; it now becomes relativized to being *one* of the societies which so functions. If I am a physician, I will not expect the church to give or to be able to give me complete guidance on the proper conduct of my profession; in many respects here I will have to look to (secular) medicine. If I am a teacher, I will not expect the church fully to understand the character of and need for full academic freedom, freedom to express every viewpoint no matter how alien to the Christian message and faith; here the secular educational institutions may give me guidance and may, indeed, need to teach the church. The church will no longer be able to set itself over against all other societies in its conviction that somehow it has the full truth which has been denied the rest of humankind.

This relativizing and restricting of the church's insights and importance does not mean that compromise between one's Christian obligations and some other obligations is called for. As I asserted in the original article on "Nonresistance and Responsibility" (p. 75, above):

> There is no place for compromise in the Christian ethic, if compromise be interpreted as some kind of voluntary sacrifice of the requirements of love to enable action in some other fashion. Love is just that which has adequate resources within itself—the very resources of God himself—to make it possible to meet with and deal with every situation which it confronts in all its variety and all its sinfulness.

The relativizing of the church's authority and importance vis-a-vis the other institutions and communities in society does not mean compromise, then; rather it means we recognize that the only demand finally binding on us is *God's will,* and this never finds perfect expression in the finite demands of any given community or society, even the church. "We must obey God rather than men" (Acts 5:29, RSV) was a word first spoken to and in defiance of *religious* (not political) authority, and its significance lies precisely in its recognition that the ultimate demands laid upon us transcend every particular historical institution and community, including even the church which is attempting to lead a faithful and committed life. It is in fact only the recognition that God's will (as revealed in Christ) transcends the wishes and will of every particular historical community that enables us to balance the chaos of demands and obligations impinging upon us from the many societies in which we participate; for only this can provide us with a genuinely integrating and unifying authority by which we can live. Giving ourselves too easily and too fully to any finite authority or society—even that of the church, which has been charged with the responsibility of bearing and spreading the gospel—results only in parochialism and pride, and must finally be accounted idolatrous.

Whatever may have been the case (or the justification) with the Anabaptists, it seems clear to me that the church cannot so easily claim God's authority for her acts as most of the Reformation churches did. Doubtless this claimed authority was a consequence of the church's confidence that God really had revealed himself and really does impart his Spirit,[7] and there thus appeared to be a theological justification for it. But it seems to me that in all groups of the Reformation period (Anabaptists and other Protestants, as well as Roman Catholics) there was too little recognition that along with this confidence must go a deep awareness of our own limitations and sinfulness, and thus our tendency to corrupt God's gift to our own uses. This awareness of our own relativity is perhaps an insight gained (in God's providence) through the development of democratic institutions in the Anglo-Saxon world and through the pluralism of American culture.[8] We Mennonites, I think, have not taken it seriously enough, but we dare not ignore it, for it has theological warrant—a point continental (and continental-trained) theologians have often failed to understand. It means that we can never, in practice *or by implication,* put ourselves in the position of claiming God's authority for our own opinions, decisions, or actions. Thus the claims of and for the empirical church must be much more modest— precisely because we believe *God* is the lord of history—than we have often realized.

In actual fact, as we all know, the church's authority *has* become relativized for most of us American Mennonites. Our norms and values are shaped and our decisions heavily influenced by the Farm Bureau and the American Medical Association, Time Magazine and TV, more than by the church. In consequence there has been a breakdown in Mennonite communities of the authority of the religious tradition, and this has had and will continue to have many deplorable consequences. I have no desire to justify or defend any of this, because for the most part it represents breakdown and disintegration rather than deliberate decision on the basis of theological insight. But not everything here is to be deplored, either, for it is precisely this growth in influence of extra-Mennonite societies and currents that has opened us up to our responsibilities as a

Christian church to the outside world and has enabled us to gain some perspective on the limitations and parochialness of much traditional Mennonitism—i.e., it has made it possible for us to be more faithfully Christian. I do not say we have become more faithful; far from it. But a possibility lies before us that did not lie before our forebears, and for this we must be grateful to God.

One of the most difficult aspects of this relativizing of the church's authority among Mennonites has to do with the role of the brotherhood in individual decision making. Yoder[9] rightly criticizes my analysis of decision for regarding the church largely as part of the *context* of decision, and giving it no place in the decision-making process itself. His point is well taken. Something should have been said there, and must yet be said. But what is it to be? It seems to me anachronistic to pretend that the individual North American's (even American Mennonite's) life is lived so largely in the church community that he can meaningfully submit many of his decisions to the judgment of his fellow Christians. No individual makes decisions entirely in isolation, of course, but the actual communities that participate in our decisions now are the family, the business or professional organization, the labor organization, the nation, and for the young probably the educational institution (with its many teachers and counselors) and the peer group. I too would like to see the church play some significant role in the decisions which are so largely shaped in these other ways. But the sociological facts seem to be that *our lives are really lived out in these other connections* more than in the church, and that therefore these societies become the dominant ones in shaping our decisions. It is to the members of these societies that we turn for advice and help. How this is to be rectified, I do not know. But certainly it will not do simply to cry for a larger role for the church here. The solution can come only through the much fuller (sociological and ethical) study and discussion of the actual and the proper relation of the church to other societies, and of the individual's joint participation in several of these.

(3) *The individual Christian and the church in the world and responsible for it.* I can draw together these observations now in a brief conclusion. My critics and I agree on the Christian responsibility to witness and minister to the world, that the church cannot live to itself alone and remain a *Christian* church. In this respect we have all, I think, given up much of the stereotyped picture of traditional Mennonitism as insisting on withdrawal from society. We do not fully agree, however, on the reasons for this repudiation of withdrawal. My reasons are both theologico-sociological and theologico-moral; my critics' reasons, I think, are largely of the latter type. That is, I think that the actual nature of the church as a society in the midst of other societies (as well as the explicit requirements of

the Christian ethic) necessitates a reassessment of the relation of the church and the world in our thinking. It may well be that in earlier, less complex periods of history it was less unreasonable to think of the church and other societies as more or less autonomous organisms over against each other, each with its own life. But in our time civilization has become so complex, with all parts so intimately interrelated in multitudinous ways, that this is simply out of the question. Perhaps this means we should withdraw from twentieth-century culture entirely to establish new colonies in a world where we will not be so involved. Most of us, I suspect, are not prepared to regard that alternative either as feasible or right. We have been placed by God in twentieth-century American society, and it is our task now to find a way to live as Christians in it.

How, then, are individual and church to be understood in their relation to the institutions and communities of secular society? I think we must give up the defensive posture that sees all of the rest of society as offering some kind of competition which the church must meet and overcome, as though the church were one among a number of competitors for its members' allegiance. Such a view leads us inevitably to thinking of the church in the same terms as the others, namely as one institution (one "power-structure") among many, this being the institution in charge of the (increasingly insignificant in modern society) religious dimension of life. Mennonites have always understood the Christian faith to call for a revolution in the whole of life, not to be simply an ordering of one dimension (the religious) in it. They have seen that whereas secular society is governed by power and sin, the Christian faith speaks of a redeeming of the world precisely through God's nonresistant love. Here is a "power" that cannot be regarded as a part of the "power-struggle" in the world, for it is precisely the power which transforms that struggle of destruction and chaos into community and love. The church, then, is to be the community with nonresistant love as its basis, the community through which nonresistant love pervades the world. It cannot be this if it is simply one more institution like and alongside and in competition with the others.

Too much of Mennonite history has failed to see this implication of the Mennonite understanding of Christian faith, and has supposed it feasible simply to create a little Mennonite world outside of the evil pagan world, with the consequence that many of the evils of the outside reappeared again within. But it is not possible to create a little Christian haven alongside the great big bad pagan world. A Mennonite utopia is no more feasible in history than any other kind.

Does this mean, then, that we must capitulate to the unchristian norms of American culture? that we must let the social groups in which we participate determine the mode and quality of our lives?

Both Meyer and Habegger seem to have understood my previous article to be leaning too far in this direction, Meyer suggesting I was arguing that "when in a given situation we have to decide whether to act as citizens or as Mennonites, we should act as citizens first," with the "American nation . . . the object of [my] first loyalty,"[10] and Habegger claiming that I was limiting "'love' to the borders of the United States."[11] My point, of course, as the above has I hope made clear, is that no finite society or community—whether the American nation or the Mennonite church—should be the object of our first loyalty, that this must be reserved for God who is seeking to penetrate redemptively all such societies. It is precisely the misunderstanding of the church as a kind of society in competition with, for example, the nation, that has misled us Mennonites into utopian withdrawal, the Amish being an outstanding example. When I spoke, therefore, of helping the nation to formulate a policy in line with its own best ideals (pp. 74ff. above), I was not advocating capitulating to the moral level of the nation, but rather pointing out that to work redemptively within an admittedly non-Christian moral situation one must, in the words of an article by John Yoder, "speak to the man in terms of the ideals to which he himself commits himself."[12] We must see, that is, that there are already tendencies within the situation which are working in some measure for the good—that God has been working there redemptively even before we Mennonites arrived on the scene! And it is in terms of these tendencies that we must act and to these tendencies that we must appeal when working in non-Christian segments of the social order.

But this means that we cannot conceive "the world" (viewed now as that society outside the church) as wholly in the hands of the evil one. On the contrary, it is already being penetrated by God's redemptive love, and we who know explicitly of this love and are committed to it are called upon to enter into that world in order to help make explicit and open what is already growing, hidden within like a seed. From this point of view it is probably important for Mennonites to acknowledge—John Howard Yoder to the contrary notwith-standing[13]—that responsible leaders in the sector of which we have traditionally been most suspicious—the political order—are to be regarded more as "high-level civil servant[s]" than as among "the foremost 'princes of the world.'"

Our task is neither to redeem the world (that is God's task) nor to be a redeemed world (that is the world's task). Our task as individuals and as a church is to be the instruments through which God furthers his work of transforming the world in which we find ourselves. We become those instruments precisely at the point where we become the catalysts making it possible—in the political order, the economic order, the social order, i.e., in the world—for the better to prevail rather than the worse, for that which builds community among men to gain at the expense of the powers of oppression and destruction. As Mennonites, we believe that this transformation is ultimately wrought only by nonresistant love, not by power and compulsion, however benevolently motivated. But this does not mean that power can never have good effects—the nonviolent use of tremendous power resources by the civil rights movement has given the lie to any such view. It is to the support of and further transformation of such movements in the direction of full nonresistant love that we are called. For in just this way God's redemptive love actually penetrates and gradually transforms the evil structures of this world.

The church, then, must be penetrative of society rather than withdrawing from it; it must make itself a force working within the various social structures rather than another society alongside "the world." (This does not mean that certain strategic withdrawals from certain dimensions of society might not be made from time to time, but these would only be conceived as of a short-term sort, in order to make more effective the goal of penetration.) In saying the church must be penetrative I mean to suggest a position which, recognizing the interlacing and interlocking of all of the segments of modern culture, seeks to *follow these lines of interconnection which are already there, transforming them from power relations and connections to vehicles of redemptive love.* Thus, we should not seek to repudiate our *de facto* involvement in American society by such voluntary and relatively trivial acts as refusing to vote or hold office or influence our congressmen; we should rather seek to utilize the positions we as a matter of fact hold in the social and economic and political orders as vehicles through which some measure of God's redemptive love can flow.

To be the church in this way would be much more difficult than following the more traditional Mennonite patterns. For the practice of withdrawal had the advantage of shielding the community from norms and practices which conflicted with its own; all of the social pressures could be mobilized toward conforming to traditional (and supposedly Christian) practices and beliefs. But if the church is to become a genuinely effective agent *in the world* it will be subjected to ways of thinking and acting, to beliefs and values and convictions, to intuitions of truth and reality and goodness, sharply at odds with its own. In dealing with persons of different conviction it will become necessary to think and act with reference to those convictions as well as ours. In this living confrontation between the power structures of the world and nonresistant redemptive love, there will often be no clearly right and no clearly wrong course of action in a given concrete situation, and there will be wide room, therefore, for sharply different conclusions and decisions as to the appropriate Christian act.[14] In such complexity and such ambiguity, to hold fast to the (Mennonite) insight that God's redemption is worked through nonresistant love, while at the same time remaining a significant and effective agent of that redemption in the midst of the clash of powers which are anything but nonresistant, will be difficult indeed. Often, doubtless, there will be capitulation to the seductive claim that only power— wielded, of course, by "good" people—can be truly relevant and effective in the face of destruction and sin, and we, too, despite our long tradition will seek to accomplish God's end with the devil's shortcut. At other times, no doubt, we will yield to the ever-present Mennonite temptation to withdraw from this or that particularly repulsive evil situation or disgusting task, that God's redeeming love may be maintained in all its nonresistant holiness and purity. But we may take neither of these alternative ways, however attractive they may appear from time to time. For we are called to be the church. We are not called merely to stand at one side and preach, wringing our hands about the evils into which this world has fallen and calling for repentance that God might redeem it. We are called to be the very instrument through which nonresistant love actually enters into the power struggles and clashes in this world to redeem them.

[1] *Concern*, No. 6, A Pamphlet Series for Questions of Christian Renewal (Scottdale, Pa: Herald Press, 1958) pp. 30-39.

[2] *Concern*, No. 7 (1959), pp 33-40.

[3] *Relativism, Knowledge and Faith* (Chicago: University of Chicago Press, 1960), and *The Context of Decision* (Nashville: Abingdon Press, 1961).

[4] *Mennonite Quarterly Review* (1963) 37:133-138.

[5] *Op. cit.*, pp. 33-35.

[6] *Op. cit.*, p. 37 (italics mine).

[7] Yoder, *op. cit.*, p. 137.

[8] It will be observed here that I do not agree with Yoder (*ibid.*, pp. 136-138) that I have rejected the all-too-great authority of the church in the Anabaptist tradition in the name of the mass-church tradition; it would be more correct to say I am rejecting the common authoritarianism of both these lines in the name of "liberal" traditions rooted in the Enlightenment and modern democratic experience. The character and the theological significance of the relativism emergent from these more recent traditions, I have sketched in my book on *Relativsm, Knowledge and Faith*.

[9] *Ibid*, pp. 135, 136.

[10] *Op. cit.*, pp. 36, 37.

[11] *Op. cit.*, p. 35.

[12] "Capital Punishment and Our Witness to Government," *The Mennonite*, (June 11, 1963) 78:394.

[13] MQR, *op. cit.*, p. 136.

[14] The complexity of the act of decision and the problem of taking account of the various ambiguous factors involved in it I have analyzed above in Ch. 6. The analysis there ought to make clear that I do not identify Christian obligation with American political desires in quite such simpleminded fashion as Habegger and Meyer suggest.

# Chapter 8

# The Significance of Art*

The uniqueness of man, that which distinguishes him most sharply from the other animals, is his power to create and develop an artificial world in which he then lives, the world of culture. Unlike any other creature, man orders his life by complex institutions of law, custom, and politics; he supplies his basic needs for food and shelter through complicated economic processes, which in turn produce for him many comforts and luxuries above and beyond his actual physical needs; he stores up his experience in great libraries of information and passes on what he has learned to succeeding generations through schools and universities. In his agriculture he has learned to make the earth produce what he wants; in his mining he has uncovered materials for building virtually any kind of structure he desires; and through his development of modern industry he has succeeded in becoming the conqueror not only of the land, sea, and air which are his immediate environment, but now even the outer reaches of space are becoming subject to his continually growing power. The artificial world of civilization built by man has superceded the natural world as the environment which modern man knows as his home.

Though we Mennonites have been suspicious of the "world," we have not failed to participate in this construction of an artificial world of culture. In our work as farmers and housewives, as teachers and doctors, as engineers and more recently as scientists, we have helped to sustain civilization and contribute to its development in various directions. We have been inclined, however, to raise ethical and

*From *Mennonite Life* (1965) 20:5-7.

religious questions about participation especially in two dimensions of cultural life: the political, because of its seemingly inevitable involvement with the sword; and the aesthetic, which has seemed to us, perhaps, frivolous. There is not time here to consider the historical reasons or justification for these attitudes;[1] it is important that we see, however, that a rejection or suspicion of artistic activity rests on a misunderstanding. For art is at the basis of all culture and civilization.

This is obviously true in the sense of the original meaning of the term "art" which is simply "skill," the ability gained through practice and knowledge to achieve what one sets out to do, whether it is build a house or grow a tree or put together a tasty stew. All of a person's life, and indeed the whole of human history, can be viewed as the development of increasingly complex arts making possible the accomplishment of previously undreamed of objectives. But this means that art is really more than mere skillfulness. It is the very process through which human purposes are realized. That is, it is the way in which that which was originally within man as mere idea or desire or dream becomes externalized as an action performed or an object made; it is the means through which the private and subjective and inner becomes something in the objective and public world; it is the way in which we express ("push out") our innermost being and thus communicate and commune with our fellows. Art is human expression, and as such, the very means of communication; it is thus art that makes possible the binding of persons to each other in community.

We can see this most clearly when we remember that language is fundamentally an art and is in fact the most fundamental of all arts. When he invented language, man devised a way to make mere noises (and various physical movements and gestures) serve his own quite artificial purposes. Instead of remaining mere vibrations of the air which might terrify or soothe depending on their natural quality or intensity, they came to "stand for" or signify realities quite different from themselves: a tree, yellowness, a pain, jumping, food, joy, etc. The vast network of symbols by means of which we are enabled to think highly complex ideas, to remember the past and to imagine various possible futures, to work out plans and purposes—this whole symbolical world we take so much for granted that we may forget it is a human creation, the product of man's skill with noises and marks on paper—this is art. We can scarcely imagine what life would be without this means of thinking and expressing ourselves; it certainly would not be in any recognizable sense *human* life. In the creation and development of language is to be found the outstanding example of the way in which man has transformed aspects of the natural world in which he found himself so they could serve his purposes, thus becoming the artificial (made by art) world of culture. In so doing, of course, he has transformed himself into a cultural—and not merely a natural—being, that is, a being who could express himself, a being for whom that which is subjective and within could be made objective and public, a being who could communicate deliberately with his fellows.

Language is fundamentally art; and art is fundamentally language. That is, in all his arts man is expressing—making external and public—that which is within him, and thus through his arts he communicates with his fellows. Speech is a marvelous instrument for thought and communication, but it is, of course, limited. Why, after all, should we expect standardized noises to be perfectly adaptable to express and communicate anything and everything within us? Our world is full of colors and smells, actions and motions, purposes and resistance to our efforts, dreams and pains. To make external and public all that we experience and feel within, the widest variety of instrumentalities is required. If our spirits are genuinely to communicate with our fellows so that we can enter fully into community with them, all the arts man has been able to devise will be required. Each is capable of expressing some nuance or dimension of experience unknown to the others.

We Mennonites know this best, perhaps, in connection with the art of music. We have always enjoyed singing, and many of our congregations have fine choruses. But this has not been simply a matter of pleasure. Man cannot express his feeling of joy in, for example, the praise of God, in mere unmusical words; it is necessary to lift his voice in song. The many dimensions of sorrow and penitence, guilt and misery, can all be much more adequately shared with others in and through the mysterious power of music. The harmonies and dissonances of the chords, the changing rhythms of different beats, the melodic lines—each plays its indispensable part in enabling this art form to express and communicate something of the human spirit unknown and inaccessible to speech or writing. A poem or a prayer sung is not the same as simply spoken, for the very form of the expression transforms the content of what is expressed. A good musician is one with the ability and training and sensitivity to express with clarity and precision dimensions of our common experience which the rest of us would otherwise not notice or appreciate and certainly could not express. His art in this way clarifies and amplifies the meaning of our common life which would otherwise remain on prosaic and dull—and thus relatively empty and meaningless—levels.

What has been said of music applies equally to the other special arts. Thus, in painting and sculpture, form and color and texture become the vehicles through which dimensions of man's inner experience not expressible in any other way can be shared. The great artist is always one who through the use of particular materials can enable the rest of us to sense dimensions of life and experience which would otherwise remain vague and hidden, without which our lives would be much the poorer. The work of an artist, therefore, is not some unnecessary ornamental luxury with which we could just as well dispense. In enabling us to see and feel what would otherwise remain hidden and invisible to us, the artist helps us realize more profoundly our own humanity and the nature of the world in which we live. Through art we come to discover the sorts of people we are, the problems of our cultures and our communities, the depths of meaning in our common life.

Once we realize that all art is language—and thus the very stuff of human communal and cultural existence, not some mere ornamental and unnecessary frosting for the cake—so-called modern art may become more comprehensible. For the contemporary artist is not trying to produce the "beautiful" in the sense of a kind of sweet or pleasing decoration for our lives. He is, rather, trying to reveal to us ourselves, to speak to us through his medium of dimensions of our common world which we might otherwise fail to notice or refuse to observe. Thus, if Tennessee Williams' plays powerfully portray the ugliness of dishonest, crude, and destructive relations between persons, we should not criticize Williams for dwelling on the seamy side of life instead of giving us a picture of superficial happiness and peace. We should rather thank him for helping us to see more clearly and vividly the terrifying inhumanity and wickedness in our slick and "civilized" culture and in our own souls. If in Picasso's paintings twisted and contorted faces, human bodies broken to pieces, and images of chaos appear, instead of disdaining what seems to us the disorder of his painting, we should ask whether he has not reflected and expressed in an especially vivid and profound way the destructive horror of the actual world in which we live, which tears people to shreds in atomic war and death camps and racial hatred. If much modern painting and modern music has become so abstract that the colors seem to us to have no order or meaning and the dissonant sounds break upon our ears as sheer noise, we may ask ourselves whether life in modern industrial America has not become so sterile and abstract as to be virtually empty of meaning and whether, therefore, this does not in fact faithfully represent to us what we are and what we live for. Moreover, in all these cases were we to look less superficially we might well discover that the artist has uncovered beyond the chaos or abstraction which he depicts some hidden order and form and meaning which we had failed to see before and which we would never have seen without his prior vision. In every generation the art forms lay bare the meaning of the lives of those in that generation. If we find ourselves preferring the music of Bach to that of Bartok, or the painting of Rembrandt to that of Rouault, this is perhaps an indication of our unwillingness to face the harsh realities of life in the twentieth century and a secret desire to live in some supposedly more tranquil or easier time. The contemporary artist, as one who is especially skilled in making the materials of experience—color, shape, sound, rhythm, speech, action—express openly and publicly what is within us, can reveal to us our lives and our world, and thus our very selves. If we wish to know ourselves profoundly and not falsely, we had better listen carefully to what the artist is saying to us through his medium.

It is possible to tie together what I have been saying with an explicit word about the religious significance of art and about so-called religious art. I have been arguing that art is not a kind of separate and perhaps unnecessary realm of culture, but that it is the activity at the base of all culture and all community, the activity of expression and communication. Without it, therefore, our life would be less than human. Everyone engages in art each time he speaks or acts and thus externalizes that which would otherwise remain a mere vague and formless inner feeling. The "artist" (in the narrower more ordinary sense of the word) is one who is able to create words or other forms which express and communicate with more precision or more profundity or more sensitivity. Far from being a dispensable luxury, the artist is the servant of us all at the deepest level of our needs as selves and communities. In this sense of dealing with the most profound levels of life and experience, all art has an important religious function. For it is through works of art that we discover what is the really "ultimate concern" (Tillich) of a culture or a generation, what are the gods or idols really worshiped there. It is through their art that people betray their real faith, whether it is in God or in some other. In this sense the most "secular" painting or "profane" play is of religious significance.

Art that takes as its symbolic vehicle a "religious" subject, such as Christ, or the creation of mankind, or the last judgment, may of course have a further religious significance, either positive or negative. For here the artist is attempting to use the symbols and forms believed by the community to express its deepest faith, to throw light and understanding on certain dimensions of the life of that society. If words about sin and salvation, or images of a cross or of God's fatherly love, authentically express the deep strata of the existence of that community, then a piece of authentically religious art may be produced; and the work of art will become a further vehicle of genuine faith in God, itself enhancing and deepening the faith of those who see or hear it. For many, Bach's music, or in our own day, Rouault's painting, has this quality and power. On the other hand, if these religious symbols are used in a spuriously religious or merely sentimental way—as in such contemporary paintings as Sallman's "Head of Christ" and such tepid and phony "religious" novels or movies as *The Big Fisherman* with their saccharin sweetness and artificiality—the very symbols are degraded and their religious power is only further weakened and destroyed. For the faith that they express and inspire is merely sentimental feeling, not the substantial stuff on which real life in this hard world can be built. Such art is mere decoration, not the very substance of life. "Secular" or "profane" art that honestly expresses the actual existence in which we find ourselves is more authentically *religious* than this dishonest and superficial art which misuses "religious" subject matter and symbols.

Art is of great importance to the church—not because the church needs fancy ornaments or nice doodads here and there but because the church is our community of faith, and if we are to live as people of faith in that community, we must learn to discern and to express and to communicate both the many dimensions of our lives and this faith. It is art in its several forms that makes such discernment and such communal life possible. But art—the expression of life—can also be false and misleading and deceiving, and can thus be destructive of our common life and faith. It is important, therefore, that we learn to cultivate and appreciate truly good art in its various forms, and that we encourage those artists and potential artists in our churches to develop and educate their special gifts. For theirs are the eyes which will finally enable us to see with genuine insight who we are and in what our life really consists; theirs are the creative spirits which can give us the words and other symbols with which to express and communicate our life and faith. Without their work Christian faith as understood within the Mennonite church cannot grow or even survive as a living faith in the modern world.

[1]For a discussion of the problem of art in Mennonite history, see *Mennonite Encyclopedia,* article on "Art," Vol. I, pp. 165-172.

# Chapter 9

# Mennonites and Professionalism*

For too long we Mennonites have allowed the modern world simply to overtake us, and have not attempted carefully and intelligently to assess what was happening. In consequence, for the past two generations there has been a steady flow of our young people from the rural communities in which they were raised into cities where they have been swallowed up and lost. Even though we have established churches in many of the larger cities to which Mennonites have gone, we have seldom systematically reflected on the question of what happens to the traditional Mennonite style of life and ethics in a modern urban environment. So our urban churches have been, as far as possible, simply transplanted rural Mennonite churches in character and quality; or they have taken over, rather unthinkingly, patterns of life and ministry from other groups with quite different understandings of Christian faith than those characteristic of Mennonites. The question of how the Mennonite interpretation of Christian faith can be relevant to modern urban and professional life has seldom been faced directly.

I want to acknowledge immediately that I am no expert on this problem. I am a Christian theologian of Mennonite background who has lived most of his life largely outside of Mennonite community circles, one who has been involved, as a professional, in American university education. This background (as a Mennonite), this vocation (reflecting on the meaning of Christian faith), this

---

*Delivered at a Conference on Mennonites and Professionalism in Philadelphia, Pa., March, 1978.

experience (as a member of a major "profession" in modern America), and my personal concern about the meaning of the Mennonite heritage in the modern world are my only qualifications for speaking to this subject. My own ideas here should be treated as, at best, just tentative formulations of what seem to me to be some of the problems confronted by bearers of the Mennonite heritage when they move into the modern professional world.

I do not intend in this essay to take up the problems of particular professions, or to give a profile of what modern professionalism is all about. I shall confine myself to the attempt to isolate and analyze certain features of our Mennonite heritage which, it seems to me, present particular problems for those moving into the highly educated modern professional world. And I shall attempt to suggest the sort of reformulation of Mennonite-Christian faith that seems to me required if we are to meet adequately these issues.

## I.

How does it happen that there is a special problem for Mennonites who become professionals? What sort of problem is it? I am no sociologist, but I think some sociological remarks might be in order here to set the stage for our more theological considerations. Throughout most of their history, Mennonites (excepting those in Holland) have lived in relatively closed, relatively small rural communities. Everyone knew everyone else; everyone lived substantially the same style of life, faced the same problems, cherished the same values. Though some Mennonites went into so-called helping professions like teaching or medicine, these seemed to be direct expressions of the basic Mennonite understanding that life is to be devoted to the service of one's fellow human beings. Certainly, the beginnings of professionalized life in small communities did not seem to raise serious questions with the Mennonite communal ethic.

The situation for those of us in modern urban professions is very different from this. We no longer live as members of relatively closed, small communities, sharing a common ethos and lifestyle with all our neighbors; we are now more or less isolated individuals in large cities, working in a variety of vocations, including highly specialized professions, and dealing with increasingly complex, unprecedented problems. Most of our contacts are with others who do not share our understanding of Christian faith and who may be pursuing very different values than we think appropriate. The problems on which we and our colleagues in the several professions have to make decisions raise issues that human beings have never thought of before, and for which our Mennonite traditional ethic has given us virtually no preparation at all. If we are physicians, we must concern ourselves with questions like when, and under what circumstances, it is right for us to perform abortions, or whether our patient is truly "dead," so that it is legitimate to remove an organ for transplant. If we are lawyers or politicians, we must be prepared to write and assess laws that will define under what circumstances that abortion will be legitimate and legal, or how certain businesses ought to be regulated so as to protect consumers, or what American policy ought to be with regard to Israel or South Africa. If we are in business, we must face the question whether all investments are equally legitimate, what degree and kind of "truth" we will present in our advertising, what kind of labor policies are appropriate and just in today's world. One could go on and on. Whether we are architects, teachers, psychiatrists, or bankers, new and exceedingly difficult moral dilemmas are bound to face us. For many of these our traditional Mennonite background has given us no preparation whatsoever. Moreover, for many of these our fellow professionals have no more wisdom than we on how to proceed.

The problem is more acute for us Mennonites than for many of our professional friends, however, because of a peculiarity of the Mennonite consciousness: the notion of the church as set over against the world. Mennonites have what the sociologists often call a sectarian consciousness. We tend to see the world outside the church as sinful, fallen, dangerous; it is inside the Christian community that right and truth are to be found, and it is from the Christian community, therefore, that one is to take one's principal orientation in life. This sort of closed-group consciousness worked satisfactorily as long as Mennonites lived in relatively closed communities where they could insulate themselves fairly successfully from the outside world. But in modern professional life it makes no sense at all. Our lives are lived for the most part outside the confines of the church. Our professional education is acquired from schools that have little interest in or knowledge of Mennonite traditions, and that means that the very form of our professional life will be "worldly." Almost everything we do as professionals we do as participants in secular institutions that have little or no interest in the church. It is therefore impossible for modern Mennonite professionals to live the church-world dualism which characterized an earlier period of Mennonite history. If we are going to be professionals today, our lives will be lived "in the world" in a much fuller sense than many earlier Mennonites would have regarded as legitimate, and the norms and standards in terms of which we make decisions in our professions will be drawn from our experience in the world. The major sociological assumptions on which earlier formulations of Mennonite faith were based simply do not hold true for modern professional life.

Does this mean that if one is to be a professional in the modern world one cannot be a loyal Mennonite? Or that if one is a convinced

Mennonite, he or she dare not go into a modern profession? I take it that it is the pressure of questions like these that lie behind the convening of this conference.

## II.

The problems which our Mennonite heritage poses as we confront the modern professional world go considerably deeper than the much too simple church-world dualism I have just mentioned. They are rooted, I think, in some of the most fundamental Mennonite convictions about the foundations of our moral knowledge, in our understanding of life itself.

Most human beings seldom ask questions about where their moral ideas and insights come from. We acquire ideals of honesty, loyalty, justice, and mercy along with a great deal else in the way of knowledge, habits, and skills as we grow through childhood and adolescence to maturity. For the most part human values and ideals are learned in the family and in the immediate community in which one grows up. The tradition which informs the life and institutions of that community becomes the tradition which we make our own and thus which comes to orient our life. This is true whether we are Americans or Chinese, Christians or Hindus, Mennonites or Jews or secularists. As long as it is possible for a community to maintain patterns of life similar to those which had been followed in the past, the tradition can remain viable and significant as a means of orientation for members of the community, and it is not necessary to search for new standards or values to guide one's decisions. Moral practice and understanding can follow long-tested habitual patterns.

It is when persons encounter quite new situations, forcing them to deal with unprecedented problems, that the tradition gets called into question. At those moments where the traditional maxims and habits no longer seem to apply, one is forced to ask in a new way about right and wrong, what shall I do, how shall I plot my course. Then one moves back to what one believes to be the sources of moral insight or moral understanding in order to gain a standing place from which to address the new and complex issues. Perhaps one will turn to the philosophical tradition of moral reflection, to see what can be learned there about rightness and goodness and justice. Or perhaps one will turn within, listening for a clearer word from the voice of conscience. Or again: one may turn to others alleged to be wise persons—counselors, pastors, teachers—who may give one guidance.

For Mennonites, the source of moral insight and understanding has been believed to be the Scripture. The Bible, and particularly the teachings of Jesus, have been thought to present the very "word of God"—the absolute truth about right and wrong, the perfect norm for ordering all of human life. When traditional patterns and practices no longer seemed relevant, therefore, Mennonites have believed they should turn back to the Scripture to resolve their problems. Here they would find guidance enabling them to deal with the new issues which faced them.

Thus, the basic Mennonite orientation in life has been *authoritarian*. Mennonites have believed that there is an absolute authority which can and does provide sufficient guidance for every situation and condition into which a human might fall. Life is based first of all on the authority of tradition, and when the traditional patterns prove no longer to be adequate, one turns back to the absolute authority of Scripture to resolve problems. If you look into the brochure announcing this present conference on "Mennonites and Professionalism," you will find the first question which it is said this conference will focus on is: "Are there any biblical principles that apply to professionalism?" Mennonites have come almost instinctively to approach new problems with that sort of question as the first to be addressed.

Now I want to suggest that the movement into professional life with which we are concerned in this conference is one which calls into question—perhaps renders obsolete—precisely this traditional Mennonite turning to authority, as the appropriate way to deal with new problems in life. The simple and straightforward Mennonite beliefs about the Bible's authority are called into question in at least two ways for those who have a modern professional education. In the first place, a member of a modern profession will ordinarily have a liberal arts college education and several years of university training beyond that. Such a person, knowing something of modern history and science, will be aware that the Bible was produced in a culture very different from our own, that it presents many ideas about the world, about human existence, about the movements of history, that we can only regard as mythical, and that it is in many respects a culturally relative product of a particular segment of human history. However important the Bible may have been as formative of Western culture—and it was very important indeed—any modern educated person now sees it as relative and limited in many respects. Aware as we are of the at least equal importance that Greek traditions have had in forming our culture, and of the several other religiocultural traditions which humankind has produced around the world, it becomes increasingly difficult to regard the Bible as the kind of absolute authority which it was for our parents and grandparents. The very education, thus, which one undergoes in preparing for a modern profession tends to undercut, or call into question, the relatively naive belief in biblical authority which has characterized much Mennonite faith. One begins to wonder in what sense, and why, one can claim this particular document to be somehow the very "word of God," having a kind of absoluteness that other monuments of ancient wisdom cannot claim.

It is not his or her education alone, however, which tends to erode biblical authority for the modern professional. Even more serious is the fact that the Bible seems to have no clear word on many of the important issues that one has to face in one's professional life. Doubtless the biblical principle of loving one's neighbor is of great importance: but what specific guidance does this give the social worker in counseling a thirteen-year-old girl on whether she should abort the three-month-old fetus that she is carrying? Of what help can the Bible be to a mortgage officer of a bank when he is attempting to formulate investment policy? What biblical principles are to be invoked if I am attempting to decide whether or not to give my life to the study of astronomy? Does the principle of love of enemy provide any specific guidance to a lawyer who has been asked to sue an unscrupulous landlord in behalf of a tenant whose apartment has been left unrepaired? The problems with which members of modern professions must deal most of the time simply were not addressed by the writers of the Bible, because they are problems that arise from a completely different cultural situation, one that those writers could never have imagined. Whatever overriding moral and religious significance the teachings of the Bible may have had for earlier generations, it is not at all clear how the Bible can remain authoritative in the day-to-day decisions of the lives of most Americans in professions.

In consequence of these two considerations—on the one hand, our increasing awareness of the actual historical process which produced the Bible and its consequent cultural relativity, and on the other hand, our increasing experience of complex and difficult moral issues to which the Bible does not seem to speak at all—biblical authority over the whole of life tends inevitably to become seriously eroded for anyone in a modern profession. Therefore as long as Mennonites insist on framing their interpretation of Christian faith in authoritarian terms, they will be in serious trouble in dealing with problems of modern urban life. An authoritarian approach to the problems of faith and life works as long as the authority is both unquestioned and obviously relevant. When either or both of those conditions is eroding away, the authoritarian approach itself is in serious danger and must be replaced by some other. If the only truly relevant and informed approach to the actual questions with which one has to deal is that found in professional journals or the public press, it is to them that the concerned person will have to turn. And with that turning, one leaves the Mennonite tradition one step further behind.

As you can see, I do not think traditional Mennonitism, rooted as it is in biblical authoritarianism, is equipped to deal with problems faced by persons in modern professions. If our Mennonite-Christian faith is to have a bearing on these issues, its very foundations must be reformulated. I would like to propose such a reformulation now.

### III.

The fact that we can no longer work out of an authoritarian biblical ethic does not mean that all that we have learned under the tutelage of that ethic is invalid. On the contrary, I am prepared to argue that the understanding of human life, its central problems, and the treatment for those problems, which Mennonites have gained from the Bible— particularly from the teachings and example of Jesus—remains valid and true, and can be the basis for dealing with problems arising in the modern professions. The professions are, after all, attempting in some way to deal with the meaning and fulfillment of human life, and any insight that can be thrown on those questions will be of immense importance in setting directions and proposing objectives for the professions.

There are three things particularly about the Mennonite-Christian understanding of the nature and meaning of human existence that I want to emphasize here. First, that human life is primarily communitarian. Human beings are not isolated atoms who can and should live unto themselves and can find fulfillment by themselves; we are members one of another, and human life finds its fulfillment in the love and trust and mutual support experienced in community. Second, genuine community is no easy achievement among human beings, each of whom is striving to gain his or her own private objectives. Rather, it is created only through the willingness of selves to sacrifice themselves for others in ministries of reconciliation and forgiveness and service, ministries that extend not only to those with whom we are in agreement but even to our enemies. The willingness to give oneself in love to one's enemies, even as Jesus gave himself on the cross, is the only kind of stance that will make possible the building of true community among humans. Third, human life is life "under God." That is, human beings, neither as individuals nor as communities, exist simply of themselves or for themselves, but they have their lives from beyond themselves, and they can find genuine fulfillment only in significant relation to that ultimate Source of their being which we call God. Life oriented toward self, life oriented toward our community or nation, even life oriented toward the good of all humanity has ultimately too narrow a focus. It is idolatrous, and as such stultifying and destructive, not only of ourselves and our fellow humans, but also of the rest of life and, indeed, of all of creation—as the ecologists are daily reminding us. If we are to live in harmony and peace with our neighbors and with the rest of creation, we must learn to devote ourselves to that One who creates and sustains us all.

These notions of love and self-sacrifice, reconciliation and community, devotion and service to God, which have been of importance to Mennonites (as well as other Christians) were learned by them under tutelage of biblical authority. And many Mennonites, I suppose, take these to be important only because they are taught in the Bible. That authoritarian position, however, is not the only possible one. It is also possible to hold to these convictions simply because one believes them to be true—true, that is, to what human nature actually is, true to the human condition, a true understanding of human problems. We are human beings, each of us, and we are daily in contact with other human beings. On the basis of our experience, and our insight into that experience, we may see how important it is for humans to love each other, to forgive each other, to live in community with each other, to worship only that God who is beyond all the idols which attract us. In that case these things are now affirmed and believed and practiced because our own insight and understanding and experience show us their significance and truth. Here it is our own understanding and insight that have become authoritative for us, the guide and basis of our judgments in life; we have moved beyond dependence on the external authority of the Bible. We are still affirming a Mennonite-Christian ethic and faith, but no longer one based simply on authoritarian foundations.

It is this kind of Mennonite approach to the problems of the vocations that I would advocate. When we recognize that our decisions will have to be based on our own insight and understanding, that we cannot depend for final answers on authorities who simply give them to us, but must take responsibility for ourselves and our judgments and our decisions, we will move to a new level of maturity. We will be open to facing whatever issues and problems confront us, examining them in their own terms, and working out as best we can a responsible approach to them. We will be prepared to learn from other professionals what they have to teach us about the issues which we must face together with them, but we will not find ourselves impelled simply to take over what they say without careful scrutiny in terms of our understanding of what human life is really all about. This does not mean that we will find easy answers to the questions we confront. But it does mean we can openly and straightforwardly confront any question we encounter, whether there are relevant biblical teachings with regard to it or not, whether Mennonites have ever looked at that issue before or not.

The approach which I am advocating allows a kind of openness and freedom in addressing problems which is virtually unlimited. It allows us—indeed, it requires us—even to be willing to question our own principles, lest they become idols which we serve instead of God. Take, for example, the central Mennonite belief that serving others, nonresistance, should characterize our every stance in life. However significant and true this Mennonite belief in self-sacrifice may seem to us, it is important for us to consider carefully the kind of evidence that persons like Nietzsche and Freud have produced against it. It seems clear that attitudes and practices of self-sacrifice are often engendered by fear instead of love, and that they can have as their consequence repressed hostility, which is anything but forgiving. All of us know from our own experience, I suspect, how frequently the tight-lipped martyr is to be found in the typical Mennonite community. Supposing it immoral ever to express hatred or hostility, many Mennonite communities are filled with tensions, bitterness, back-biting, and secret struggles for power. If the Mennonite emphasis on love and reconciliation is to be maintained, it will have to be qualified by a careful appropriation of what modern psychiatry can teach us about the deviousness and the depths of human selves. Other examples of the way in which our conceptions of human life and its fulfillment must be brought into confrontation with other traditions and points of view in the modern world could be cited: the significance of the body and of human sexuality has been little understood in traditional Mennonitism; the role of power in human institutions, including our own Mennonite institutions, has been systematically obscured; the need for beauty, and the importance of the arts in a fulfilled human life, has simply not been realized. On these and many other questions about human life, and what human life is all about, the Bible has no clear answers, and to insist on biblicism will itself be idolatrous. We must take the responsibility for our judgments on ourselves, relying on our own insight, understanding, and experience, to find such answers as we can live by and work with. We must be prepared to open up our Mennonitism to attitudes and practices unknown or even rejected in the past, in order to help enable it to become a vital and significant force in the new situation in the present in which we are living and into which we are moving.

There is, of course, some point at which transformation of the tradition has become so drastic and far-reaching that it is no longer recognizably Mennonite. Each of us would probably mark that point somewhat differently, but for all of us it is there. For my part, I would define this point, not in terms of any idiosyncratic details of Mennonite custom or consciousness, but in terms of the central vision of the human, and the fulfillment of the human, which has gripped the Mennonite consciousness: that it is in relationships of love and trust and self-giving in the reconciling community that true humanity is realized, and that the image of Jesus in ministry, teaching, and death is the criterion or paradigm in terms of which this conception of the human is concretely pictured and defined. So long as we hold to this, it seems to me, we are maintaining what is truly important in historic Mennonitism.

An approach such as I am suggesting here leaves us open to deal with whatever problems arise in the course of our professional lives. Recognizing that there are no "pre-prepared" answers to the moral and religious questions we are facing and will face, we must take responsibility upon ourselves to work out such answers as we can find. This is, so far as I can see, the only way it will be possible to be a Mennonite in a modern profession. In Philippians 2 Paul makes a similar point. First he commends the example of Jesus who, ". . . though he was in the form of God, did not count equality with God a thing to be grasped, but emptied himself, taking the form of a servant" (Phil. 2:6, 7, RSV). Then he suggests that the Philippians must now ". . . work out your own salvation with fear and trembling; for God is at work in you, both to will and to work for his good pleasure" (2:12, 13). In the last analysis, in Paul's view, even with the biblical image of true humanity before us, we must ourselves take responsibility for how this applies to our own situation, and we must act on that responsibility.

The very open and unstructured interpretation of Mennonitism in the face of modern professional life, which I am proposing, is frightening and it will be difficult to execute. It is frightening because it admits openly that there is no authority to which we can turn to resolve our most difficult moral and religious problems; it acknowledges that we must take full responsibility on ourselves in these matters. It is difficult to execute because the lack of ultimate authority means there are no clear guidelines to be followed; we will have to find our own way, and that will require both considerable time and effort and may be frustrating and exhausting. But there are resources to which we can turn for help in our reflection: above all, the picture of Jesus which we find in the Scriptures is such a resource, providing illumination of the nature and problems of human life and of the will of God whom we worship. The long history of Christian reflection on the meaning of Jesus' life, teachings, and death can provide important guidance and help in grasping the full significance of this figure central to Christian faith. Philosophical reflection on ethical issues may give us insight into important dimensions of the problems we face, and sociological analyses and literary portrayals of the complexity and problems of modern urban civilization will surely sharpen our discernment and deepen our understanding of the many layers and dimensions of the moral and religious issues with which we must deal. Finally, the efforts of some of our contemporaries in the professions in which we are living and working, to discern and interpret the moral issues at stake in the major questions facing the profession, will surely be of help. We must draw on all these resources and any others which become available to us as we seek to develop our own insight and understanding so that we can decide and act wisely and responsibly.

## IV.

If we were to attempt to go this route simply as individuals—and that is what has been forced onto many of us—I suspect we would lose our Mennonitism in the end. If not we ourselves, then our children would. There is, however, an alternative to a strictly individualistic approach, an alternative suggested by our Mennonite heritage itself. We can band together in the cities as small Mennonite communities, communities of fellow-seekers, fellow-professionals, attempting to support and help each other. If we could find a way to organize our urban churches as genuine "communities of discernment," which would seek to help their members more adequately face the unprecedented problems and decisions which modern professionals must address, there would be some chance that in the brave new world into which we are moving we would not simply become lost.

We all need a group with whom we can share our deepest and most destructive dilemmas; we need a group so open and nonjudgmental that we can bring our most secret doubts and questions for discussion and consideration; we need a fellowship of love and trust where we need not deceive or cover up any of the issues that we encounter as we try to bring to bear the understanding of human existence which we have inherited from our Mennonite tradition on the problems we face in our modern professions. All too often, I fear, our Mennonite churches have been anything but open communities of this sort of love and trust. But in such open communities it might be possible for us to find truly significant Mennonite ways to face the problems posed by modern urban life. Participation in such communities might enable us finally to grow out of that childish immaturity that must always live from parental or traditional authority, gradually learning to take full responsibility for ourselves, our beliefs, and our actions. We would then ". . . no longer . . . be children" but would be moving into . . . "mature manhood, measured by nothing less than the full stature of Christ" (Eph. 4:13, 14, NEB).

# Chapter 10

# A Vision For a Mennonite College*

The lives of persons and of their communities do not proceed on an even keel. There are, of course, moments and years that move forward with little interruption or turmoil, when patterns of life developed in the past seem fully satisfactory for the foreseeable future. But there are other times when it is necessary to pause, reflect on the past and its meaning, and lay a new course for the future. Such a time as this is now upon us Mennonites.

Our life in coming generations is clearly going to be very different from what it has been the almost four and a half centuries of our past. No longer will we be an essentially rural people, more or less isolated from the world, living out our lives as pious and productive farmers; we are rapidly becoming city folk, participant in all dimensions of modern American culture at study or work in secular institutions, spending most of our waking hours in the company of those who know nothing about Mennonite principles and care less. It may be that as a distinctive group we will simply die out in the new world into which we are moving, that we have no real place there, that our time as a particular people has come to its end. No one knows whether this is our destiny and no one knows whether it would be good or evil if it were; but we all know, I think—and we face this with some trepidation—that this is a distinct possibility. It may be that we as Mennonites have some special mission to perform in the coming years for the Christian church at large and for the world, that our

*Delivered at the inauguration of Orville L. Voth as eighth president of Bethel College, North Newton, Kansas, on 5 February 1967.

unique past and our peculiar understanding of the Christian faith has prepared us for a task for which no others are similarly equipped. Again, none of us knows whether this is the case or not; but if it is, we dare not miss our calling, either through blindness or through unwillingness to accommodate ourselves, our way of life, our thinking and our attitudes, to what is required of us. It is essential, then, that we seek to understand the meaning of our past, what we have been and are, and that we open ourselves to the present world in which we live, so that we may, hopefully, better discern what is our proper work in the future that is opening before us.

It is fitting that we should consider these issues on the occasion marking the transition to new leadership of the oldest Mennonite institution of higher learning. It is fitting because our colleges have been the context, more than anywhere else, within which Mennonites have met and self-consciously grappled with modern culture. On the one hand, as centers of learning and culture, our colleges have kept before us the best of western civilization and modern life, and have thus been the point at which contemporary culture has made a living impact on our people; on the other hand, as institutions of *Mennonite* culture and learning, our colleges have fostered research into and reflection upon our Anabaptist-Mennonite past, and have thus been largely responsible for our growing awareness and understanding of the deeper significance of the values and emphases found in that past. The Mennonite church owes more than she can ever say to her colleges which have in this way provided a context within which hundreds of her young people could encounter modern culture while simultaneously being led to reflect upon and to appreciate the best of their Mennonite heritage. And it is on Bethel and her sister institutions that the church will have to depend for the foreseeable future to provide both the location for the continuing interchange of Mennonite tradition and the modern world, and the body of intelligent and committed and highly trained men and women, who can together promote such reflection in the service of the church. It is appropriate, therefore, that we should consider these issues upon the inauguration of a new college president.

But it is especially fitting that we should consider these problems of the Mennonite community here at Bethel College, the oldest of our institutions of higher learning and by common consent the one most liberal in the past. For the problems to be faced in the coming years will be far more demanding than heretofore. Before it always seemed that Mennonites had a choice: they could become educated and move out into the modern world (and thus possibly lose their faith, as the conservatives continuously warned), or they could remain home in the sheltered rural community, preserving the values and way of life of their forebears. College education seemed to many an unnecessary luxury, indeed a threat to the "simple life" which they thought to be the essence of Mennonitism. Thus, if the liberalizing of tradition which was occurring in the colleges, and their accommodation to the modern world, failed to produce a viable form of Mennonitism, one could still expect that the traditions would be preserved and conserved in the close-knit rural communities. But that choice is gone. The relatively closed communities no longer exist: modern American culture is everywhere. It is not even economically feasible to sustain life in the earlier relatively isolated and simplistic way. Church-centered life, governed principally by religious sanctions of the traditional sort, is clearly out of the question for the future. Hence, the reinterpretation of tradition and the adaptation to the modern world long advocated and practiced by our more liberal colleges is no longer an optional luxury for Mennonites; it is the only possible way in which the Mennonite church can survive as a distinctive Christian communion.

Of course, it may well be that there is no good reason for her survival, that she can just as well dissolve into the "melting pot" of general American culture. But if the Mennonite brotherhood has been preserved for these four and a half centuries for something more significant than just a final petering-out, if she has something to give to church and world at large, then she has only one option: to find her uniquely Mennonite role in specifically modern, urban, complex cultural life. The choice to which our colleges long since have pointed as right for Mennonites has now become the only one. If we fail now on the task at which they have long been working, we will have failed absolutely and with finality. And there will be nothing further to be said; indeed, there will be no Mennonites left to say it. Bethel College can be proud that she was the first among Mennonite institutions clearly to recognize the problem and first to attack it boldly. By now, I trust, it is clearly visible to all—and that therefore the constituencies of our colleges will support them both with more sympathy and understanding, and also with the requisite funds to carry through their task. We simply have no other institutions than these which can face the momentous problems confronting us as a church. We must give the colleges both the utmost freedom to define and refine the issue facing us as a Mennonite brotherhood and full support in carrying through their programs.

If the Mennonite colleges are indeed the only institutions that can possibly provide the setting for thinking through and educating for the mission of the church in the modern world, it will be necessary for them to grasp clearly this their vocation and mobilize themselves accordingly. It will not be enough for them to think of themselves simply as "Christian liberal arts colleges" like many others across the nation, with a more or less Christian ethos on campus and a more or less religiously committed faculty. Nor would it be proper for these schools to regard themselves simply as "church-related"—as largely secular institutions with largely secular functions, which, however, derive support from the church and provide a setting within which religious activities and convictions are encouraged to flourish more or less voluntarily. A Mennonite college in the contemporary world has a much more specific task than that. She is an arm of the church and she must perform certain functions for the church. In certain ways these outweigh in significance her functions as a liberal arts college, though they do not exclude that general educative task and, indeed, would be impossible apart from it.

First, Mennonite institutions of higher learning (both colleges and seminaries) must understand themselves as charged especially with the task of investigating fully and thinking out thoroughly the meaning of Mennonite faith for modern life and the work of the Mennonite church in the modern world. At no other places do we have assembled together the necessary brains, commitment, knowledge, and imagination for this task. Second, the Mennonite colleges must provide for the education of the young in this vision which they gradually evolve.

Doubtless, our Sunday schools and young people's societies, church papers and special conferences, can do much to help and supplement here. But these for the most part have presupposed the old pattern of a fairly tight communal and family life as the location within which Mennonite ideals would be largely inculcated. With those closed communities and deeply convinced families now largely gone, it is dubious that such occasional and erratic methods of religious education can possibly produce the kind of deep conviction that is necessary to a faith which goes counter to the pressures of the surrounding world in so many ways. What is needed is a setting where concentrated consideration of and reflection upon the meaning of radical Christian faith can occur, a setting in which it is enunciated with full awareness of the many dimensions and full significance of modern culture, and thus with a deep conviction regarding a mission to that culture. Many of our children are now being raised in what are predominantly non-Mennonite communities, and the pressures upon them in school and out are in directions opposite to our understanding of the extreme demands of Christian faith. A Mennonite college—a college which understood its peculiar task as grappling with the role of such radical Christian faith in the modern world—would be a setting where such young people could seriously consider the meaning of this faith for their own lives and future. In this way such a college might fulfill the function carried out in earlier generations by the more tight-knit Mennonite communities. But with a very important difference: *this* Mennonite community would be oriented not upon itself, but toward the outside world which it would be seeking to serve; it would not be parochial and narrow in its understanding of the Christian faith, but liberal and directed toward the world at large.

It is clear that only a first-rate college could perform such functions for the church. The encounter with contemporary culture cannot occur unless the arts and sciences are present in excellence, and certainly education of Mennonite youth to participate in modern life will simply fail if it is not governed by real proficiency and understanding of the sciences and arts dominant in the modern world. I am not suggesting, then, that some sort of stuffy churchy institution is what is wanted. Any school that sought to fulfill the role I am here envisioning would need real strength in all the traditional liberal arts so that her students could go into the world with a training second to none. Only such a school could attract a faculty good enough to do the kind of hard and diversified thinking about the Mennonite tradition and the modern world which desperately needs doing; only such a school could attract the most promising Mennonite youth and challenge them with an understanding of the contemporary world and the relevance of Christian faith to its deepest problems; only such a school could thus become the kind of intellectual center that the Mennonite church needs in order to make a profound and significant contribution to our world. Such a college would need to manifest the highest degree of academic strength and intellectual vigor, but something more in addition: genuine commitment in the administration and a major block of the faculty and students to exploration of and experimentation with the resources of the Anabaptist-Mennonite tradition.

Many of us who have come out of Mennonite homes and have moved into the secular world have felt—perhaps somewhat vaguely —that the modern world and modern church badly need the stimulus and corrective which this tradition could offer. If this feeling is correct, a college which deliberately set out to explore the possibilities here could be a very exciting place both to study and to teach—for Mennonites and non-Mennonites alike—and education of the highest order would take place. If this feeling is incorrect, and the Anabaptist-Mennonite past has little to offer the modern world as it faces its unprecedented problems, then it were just as well if the Mennonite church were to die. Being of no service to humankind, it would be of none to God.

Is the constituency of Bethel College prepared to allow her to become an institution of real service in this way both to church and to modern world? I do not know. It seems to me very sad that with Mennonitism facing a real crisis today, and the whole world afire with flames which we Mennonites think we know something about extinguishing, that Bethel, due to constituency pressures, still has to expend large portions of her energy on such trivial questions as smoking and dancing. And it is very sad that the administration of Bethel can count so little on Mennonite support for the school (even on the peace question), that it is not feasible to encourage student groups who wish to experiment with new forms of witness against American involvement in a highly dubious war. Unless the constituencies of our schools are willing to leave them completely free to deal with such matters as these as they see best, and unless they are willing to give full support to the faculties and students as they explore unconventional interpretations of and dramatic ways to express their Christian faith, it is of course not possible for the colleges to provide the kind of leadership which the church so desperately needs. The time is long past for the constituencies to sit in judgment on the colleges for adopting patterns of thinking and action not familiar in our conservative rural communities. The option for the church to elect that more familiar mode of life for the future is simply no longer there. The church *must* trust the faculties and administrations of her colleges, and must give them freedom to find the new mode of Mennonite existence which will be meaningful and significant for the future—or the church herself will die.

I have been putting my emphasis here on the importance of the *Mennonite* character of Bethel College. Does this mean she ought to become a strictly sectarian school, with no non-Mennonites on the faculty and few in the student body? Not at all. In this respect I think Bethel has probably been too sectarian in the past. Despite her liberal orientation, the assumption was that she was preparing young people to return to rural and semi-rural life in the mid-west Bible Belt. In consequence, the great moving forces of humanism, agnosticism, and atheism found only a small place on the campus, and seldom if ever were they given vital representation in the personal convictions of faculty members. I rather suspect that a self-proclaimed atheist would not have been given a position on the faculty. Whatever may have been the merits of such a policy in the past, it would be very nearsighted to continue to follow it. The urban civilization into which we all are being inexorably moved is a *secular* city, in which there is little interest either in God or Christian faith. We ill-prepare young people for the life they will be leading in that city if we do not confront them in college with strong representatives of the anti-Christian and non-Christian thinking and acting that is already dominant in our culture. Many of their friends and associates, for whom they will come to have great respect and affection, will take nonreligious or antireligious positions. And they should be prepared by their college experience both to understand such persons and to respect them. This is not only to assure that they will get on well with their new neighbors, nor is it to insure that they will not be seduced away from their Christian faith when they first encounter an attractive alternative. It is because education should prepare us to understand the actual world in which we are going to live and the actual lives we are going to lead, and secular humanism is in fact the dominant alternative to Christian faith in modern America. And it is because our Christian faith itself demands that we enter into the life of our neighbor, that we stand with him and beside him in sympathy and love in the life situations in which he finds himself—and the chances are that for the most part our neighbors in the future will not be Christians.

There is no excuse, then, if our colleges are to prepare young people to live in modern secular America, for them not to have strong representatives of the secular and the atheistic positions on their campuses. Indeed, it is only if these currents can be faced openly by the church in fellowship and love and dialogue that she will be able to survive in this coming world. Thus, it is precisely as *Mennonite* colleges helping the Mennonite church find its way into the unknown future that they must keep genuine intercourse between Christian faith and non-Christian positions alive on campus. In no other way would it be possible for the colleges to face up to the real problems of the coming world. To advocate, then, as I have done in this address, that our colleges become *more* pronouncedly Mennonite in orientation and purpose in no way means they should become narrower or more parochial. It means just the opposite: that the world in which we live must have active representation on our campuses precisely so the church can learn better what it is to encounter that world, for the church will no longer in the future be able to hide herself from the world about her, as she has in in the past. There must be, then, strong and vocal non-Mennonite representation on the faculty, and non-Mennonite or anti-Mennonite students should feel very much at home—though, it is to be hoped, the vitality of the radical Christian faith also present on the campus would prove a real temptation to them in their secularity.

What, now, would the kind of Mennonite college I have here envisaged look like? It seems to me there are several essentials. First of all there would have to be a clear commitment in the administration and board that this is the kind of school that was wanted. It would be necessary to decide more or less explicitly, I should think, that the Mennonite understanding of the Christian faith was worth emphasizing in this way in an institution of higher learning, and that such an institution could provide a setting within which radical Christian faith could think out its meaning and implications for life in the modern world. Only explicit commitment would lead the board and administration to think through openly and clearly what the distinctive character of such a school might be, to develop appropriate criteria for faculty appointments, for disposition of monies, for curricular emphases and student life; and only explicit commitment would prepare them to accept the difficult consequences which might well follow if the institution became a breeding ground for radical interpretations of Christian faith and correspondingly severe criticism of contemporary American culture, contemporary American values and aspirations.

Second, and equally as important as the first point, the constituency of the school—and this means the specifically Mennonite constituency—would have to be prepared to back up the institution much more forcefully and definitely than has been the case in the past with any of our colleges. No school could take the risk of so definitely identifying itself with the Mennonite tradition, a tradition rich in criticism of the accepted practices of the rest of Christendom, if it were not assured of full support, financial and otherwise, from the church, support that would take up any slack, and would help to meet the opposition that might develop from those not sympathetic to such a radical Christian emphasis. Such a school as this might have frequent crises on its hands of various sorts—the Christian faith after all, if taken seriously, is dangerous doctrine. It would be absolutely necessary for the college to know it had a constituency in full support of its programs, or it simply could not survive. Moreover, as I indicated earlier, it would not do for the churches to think they could and should be constantly looking over the college's shoulder, as it were, to see whether they approved what was being done there, and threatening to withdraw support whenever something occurred which seemed questionable, as has been the practice far too often in the past. *That* kind of support does not enable an institution to take risks, the kind of risks which a radical understanding of Christian faith would involve. No, the constituency would have to be prepared to *trust* the school even when it did not fully understand what was going on, to trust that the school was indeed working to find the way for the Mennonite church in the modern world. And it would have to be prepared to support the school out of this confidence and trust, not simply on the basis of agreement with all that transpired there. Are the Mennonite churches that founded Bethel College and who presently support her, and for whom (in the last analysis) she exists, prepared to give her this kind of support? Do they sufficiently realize the crisis of Mennonitism in the modern world to know that they must do something like this if they are to survive at all as distinctively Mennonite? I do not know.

Third, and quite as important as the first two points, the faculty of the school must be committed to the program if it is to be feasible at all. In many respects, the faculty *is* the college. It is the faculty in its daily contacts with students that does the actual teaching on the college campus; it is the faculty which determines the major outlines and character of the curriculum, and works out and presents the particular and detailed content of the courses that make up that curriculum; it is the faculty which in precept, personal conviction, and character sets the moral and religious tone of the campus, and provides, in action and life, images and examples after which students may wish to model and build their own lives and characters. An administration and a constituency may have certain objectives for a school, but only the faculty can make those objectives vital in the actual life of the school. It is clear, then, that a radically Mennonite school could not be had simply by decision of administration or support of constituency; it would also have to express the convictions of the faculty. There would have to be in the faculty a genuine interest in and a sufficient commitment to the Mennonite understanding of Christian faith to foster serious desire to think through the meaning of that faith for modern life, in the light of all the disciplines represented in the faculty. There would have to be willingness—and not only willingness but positive desire—to orient the life of the school not only to the academic disciplines in which each had been trained, but to the serious commitment to Christian faith for which the school stood.

Would this mean that every member of the faculty had to be Mennonite, regularly submitting himself to tests of orthodoxy? Absolutely not. As I have already argued, such parochialism would only defeat the whole purpose. Doubtless, a strong segment in the faculty would need to be of convinced Mennonite conviction; but the presence of other Christians, who could and would seriously question the Mennonite understanding of Christian faith, would also be needed, and secularists and nonbelievers in sufficiency of numbers and strength to give voice and example to what were the really dominant currents in contemporary American life would likewise be important. The college, to be the kind of school I am envisioning, would have to be a meeting place between Mennonitism and other significant alternative convictions and faiths, an arena where it was not already decided beforehand who was going to win in the encounter. This would demand strong non-Mennonite voices and anti-Mennonite convictions on the faculty: without such there would be no possibility of performing for the Mennonite church the task that needed to be accomplished.

Such non-Mennonite members of the faculty would of course need to understand what they were getting into—a continuing debate and discussion about the meaning of life and the convictions which ought to orient life—and they would have to be willing to participate actively in such an ongoing conversation; like the others, they would have to risk thinking through afresh their own faith and stance in the world. But beyond that nothing untoward or narrow would be required of them. I should think, if the atmosphere of the school were really open to such continuing discussion of truly vital issues as I am envisioning here, many serious faculty people with no Mennonite connections at all would welcome the opportunity to teach. Most college campuses in America today have become so antiseptically objectivistic and academic in their orientation, that many find teaching sterile and frustrating, precisely because the real issues of life and death cannot be openly expressed and discussed. It would seem to me, therefore, that it would be possible to foster in a college faculty serious and continuing discussion of those issues which to Mennonites have been important, without in any way narrowing or rendering parochial the life of the school. The widespread current disturbance in the American academic community about the war in Vietnam is sufficient evidence that the kind of issues Mennonites have long thought important are of deep significance also to many other faculty people of very different religious background and conviction. A strong faculty could be built, I think, in a school with the kind of commitments I have suggested, a faculty which would be able to present an exciting and educationally stimulating bill of fare to its students.

I have spoken about administration, constituency, and faculty. Much could also be said, of course, about the students in such a school as we are here envisioning. But it would be better, I think, not to speculate in this respect beyond suggesting that surely many of the most concerned and intelligent Mennonite and non-Mennonite students, who knew of such a school as this, would be attracted to it. Doubtless they would shape its life in important ways. But this is something that cannot well be envisioned in the abstract, because we do not know who these young folk are or what their convictions and characters are. Although, in a sense almost as important as with the faculty, the students *are* the school, in other senses they are not. It is the faculty and administration and constituency, after all, that are the relatively permanent factors constituting the school; the students come, and after at most four years, they go. It is true there is a student culture that is passed on from generation to generation, and this is a very important dimension of the school's character, but this is something which can be dealt with only by faculty and administration as they try to carry through their objectives. The purposeful and rational shaping of the quality and character of the school, therefore, can be accomplished only through those segments of the school with which we have already been concerned in these remarks. It is they who will set the objectives and develop and carry through the program for the school; and it is in accordance with the character and quality of that program that various sorts of students will be attracted to it and will thus, finally, shape and reshape the student culture there. Since the students are on the receiving end, so to speak, of the educational process, and their life is responsive to and in this sense derivative from that of the faculty, it would be inappropriate in such an address as this to attempt to speculate further about it.

Something also might be said here about the actual program of the college I am envisioning. Would special sorts of courses be offered there? If so, what would they be? Would dramatic new innovations in curriculum and teaching methods be attempted? What sort of student activities and extracurricular life would be fostered? It would be presumptuous of me—who have not taught in an undergraduate college for a good many years, and never in a Mennonite school—to attempt to answer any of these questions, and I shall not do so. Such matters must be dealt with by the faculty and administration of a school as they try to expedite their objectives. But it seems to me that the intellectual climate of the sort of college whose broad outlines I have been trying to sketch would be sufficiently invigorating, and the faculty sufficiently alive, that new and exciting methods and programs and activities would doubtless be experimented with and developed. And the total educational process in the school would have great vitality. It would be a good school at which to teach, and a good school to attend.

*    *    *

We are all moving into a brave new world, of which even the basic outlines remain unclear. With automation and the immense growth of leisure time; with worldwide events present almost instantaneously in the living room TV set, and transportation facilities that increasingly carry numbers of us to many and various far places in a matter of hours; with the population of the world exploding so rapidly that many will certainly starve in coming years; with great unrest and disorder developing throughout the world; with our own inner cities seething with resentment at continuing exploitation; with the colored peoples of the world soon to take over dominance and power from the white westerners; and, brooding over the whole, with the apocalyptic possibility now in humanity's hands to destroy all civilization and perhaps all human life through a third world war— with all this and more confronting us, it becomes trite to hammer continually at the theme that life for all of us is in for vast and unpredictable changes in the near future. Our colleges are the institutions through which we seek to prepare the coming generations for this life they will have to lead. This means that college education can no longer consist of a mere handing-over to the next generation of the treasures of the past. It must, rather, emphasize a development of openness and flexibility in its students which will, hopefully, enable them to cope with issues and problems none of us can now foresee or even imagine.

Christian faith has the advantage, in facing such an open future, of confidence that, despite whatever comes, the course of history is in God's hands, under his providential care. Indeed, faith looks to God as the One who breaks through the encrusted patterns of the old and brings the novel and unpredictable and creative into history. "Remember not the former things, . . ." says this God through the mouth of Isaiah; "Behold, I am doing a new thing. . ." (43:18, 19, RSV). "From this time forth I make you hear new things, hidden things which you have not known. They are created now, not long ago; before today you have never heard of them. . ." (48:6, 7, RSV). For faith, the course of history moves in accordance with the purposes of this God, the same God who has shown through the mode of life and the quality of death of the man Jesus that he is merciful and loving to humanity. Faith, therefore, can face this future, however threatening, however unknown, with confidence and openness and flexibility, prepared to lead whatever life is there required by God, to perform there whatever tasks contribute to the furtherance of his rule among humankind. Did we not live from such a faith as this, we could hardly look with open eyes upon all that will be demanded of us in the next generation or two, and we would be inclined to retreat blindly to our comfortable habitual patterns of life. But given such a faith, we can move out from our past, from all to which we are accustomed, into the new and unknown world which shall be ours, and there live in hope and confidence in God, in love and genuine service to our fellows. On the basis of such a faith, precisely the great challenge with which the future confronts us may call us forth into that "mature manhood . . . [that] measure of the stature of the fulness of Christ" (Eph. 4:13, RSV) which has been our proper destiny from creation.